G000270705

Elías Valiña Sampedro (1929-1989), was parish priest of O Cebreiro and Doctor of Canon Law of the University of Salamanca. Scholar and an expert on Compostelan studies, he was awarded the 'Antonia de Nebrija' Prize (1967) for his thesis *'El Camino de Santiago, Estudio histórico-jurídico'* (Madrid 1971) and the 'José María Cuadrado' Prize (1986) for the *'Catálogo de los archivos parroquiales de la diócesis de Lugo'* (Lugo 1991).

His work *'Caminos a Compostela'* (Vigo 1971) served as the prelude to *'El Camino de Santiago. Guía del Peregrino'* (Madrid 1982) for which he was commissioned as Editor by the Ministry of Tourism.

In 1984 he began the marking of the Camino with yellow arrows from the French border to Santiago de Compostela. He served as Chairman of the Committee for the first Jacobean Meeting which took place in the city of the Apostle in 1985, published a Boletín del Camino de Santiago and dedicated his efforts to the revitalisation of the Jacobean routes and to the promotion of the Asociaciones de Amigos, activities which culminated in the first International Congress at Jaca (1987).

His posthumously published work *'El Camino de Santiago, Guía del Peregrino a Compostela'* (Vigo 1992) has been translated into the principal European languages. Upon his tomb, in the pre-romanesque church of Santa María la Real at O Cebreiro, his epitaph reads:

VIAE SANCTI JACOBI INSIGNIS RESTAURATOR
ET OMNIUM PEREGRINORUM AMICUS ET FRATER

(He was distinguished for his renovation of the Way of St. James and was friend and brother to all pilgrims).

1

In memoriam
Elías Valiña

His research and his lifetime of
dedication to the Camino de Santiago.

Acknowledgement

The publisher wishes to express his gratitude for the kind co-operation of
Joseph May in the preparation of this material.

*The cover shows the stone image of the Apostle St. James as a pilgrim, carved by
Beauford Linley in memory of Elías Valiña for the pilgrim refuge at Rabanal del
Camino (León).*
Photograph by Joseph May, F.R.P.S.

The Way of St James

The Pilgrimage Route
to Santiago de Compostela

Based upon the cartography created by
Dr Elías VALIÑA SAMPEDRO

Roger Lascelles, Cartographic and Travel Publisher
47 York Road, Brentford, (Middx) TW8 0QP. Tel: 081 847 0935 Fax: 081 568 3886

Publication Data

Title	The Way of St. James
Typeface	Photoset in Garamond
Typesetting	Kelso Graphics, Kelso, Scotland
Printing	Technographic Design and Print Ltd., Essex
Photographs	Dr. Elías Valiña Sampedro and Joseph May F.R.P.S.
Maps	Computer cartography by Euromap Limited, Pangbourne (Berks.), from the original cartography of Dr. Elías Valiña Sampedro.
ISBN	1 872815 26 X
Edition	First July 1993
Publisher	Roger Lascelles 47 York Road, Brentford, Middx., TW8 OQP, UK.
Copyright	Amelia Valiña Sampedro and Pilar Armesto Valiña.

Distribution

Africa:	South Africa	Faradawn, Box 17161, Hillbrow 2038
Americas:	Canada	International Travel Maps & Books, P.O. Box 2290, Vancouver BC V6B 3W5.
	U.S.A.	Available through major booksellers with good foreign travel sections
Asia:	India	English Book Store, 17-L Connaught Circus, P.O. Box 328, New Delhi 110 001
Australasia:	Australia	Rex Publications, 15 Huntingdon Street, Crows Nest, N.S.W.
Europe:	Belgium	Brussels - Peuples et Continents
	Germany	Available through major booksellers with good foreign travel sections
	GB/Ireland	Available through all booksellers with good foreign travel sections.
	Italy	Libreria dell'Automobile, Milano
	Netherlands	Nilsson & Lamm BV, Weesp
	Denmark	Copenhagen - Arnold Busck, G.E.C. Gad, Boghallen
	Finland	Helsinki - Akateeminen Kirjakauppa
	Norway	Oslo - Arne Gimnes/J.G. Tanum
	Sweden	Stockholm/Esselte, Akademi Bokhandel, Fritzes, Hedengrens Gothenburg/Gumperts, Esselte Lund/Gleerupska
	Switzerland	Basel/Bider: Berne/Atlas; Geneve/Artou; Lausanne/Artou; Zurich/Travel Bookshop

Contents

Introduction

The Maps of the Camino de Santiago

Town Plans

The Magdalena bridge, Pamplona.

The Pilgrimage to Santiago de Compostela

'El Camino de Santiago', or Way of St. James, has been one of Europe's great spiritual, historic and scenic roads for more than a thousand years. Stretching across northern Spain from the Pyrenean border with France almost to the Atlantic, it is an 800 kilometre footpath to the city of Santiago de Compostela and the tomb of the Apostle St. James.

In 1987 the Council of Europe declared the Camino to be the first 'European Cultural Itinerary'. The physical integrity of the route and its monuments was from then on to be protected, and the journey promoted as one of the most valuable cultural experiences available to travellers, especially young people, from all countries.

Dr. Elías Valiña Sampedro, the originator of these maps of the Camino de Santiago, was the foremost modern authority on its historical and physical evolution. Until his death in 1989 he combined study and countless personal journeys along the Camino with his position as parish priest of O Cebreiro, a Galician mountain village of great importance in the history of the pilgrimage to Santiago.

Dr. Valiña was responsible for the first practical guidebooks to the route and for initially marking it with the yellow arrows that are such a distinctive feature today. His maps are the fruit of the desire to place in the hands of pilgrims a cartography of the historic Camino and its subsidiary routes, drawn to scale and in a manageable format. The result is a visual guide that is an indispensable companion for anyone making the journey to Compostela, but particularly those on foot, bicycle or horseback.

The Legend of St. James

The goal of the pilgrimage route, and the geographical and spiritual heart of the city of Santiago de Compostela, is the Cathedral that contains the remains believed to be those of St. James the Great.

The New Testament records that James was the elder brother of John the Evangelist, that both were the sons of Zebedee and Salome and were fishermen, called by Jesus Christ to become fishers of men. After Christ's death and resurrection, the apostles dispersed to carry His message throughout the world.

Santiago de Compostela cathedral: the west front.

The Puerta Santa or Holy Door, cathedral of Santiago de Compostela.

James is said to have gone to the Roman province of Hispania where he made converts and appointed bishops in León and Astorga before returning to Palestine. He was beheaded there in AD44 on the orders of Herod Agrippa – the first of the apostles to die a martyr.

James himself had followers and some of these, according to the legend, spirited his body away and set sail with it for Spain. They landed at Iria Flavia on the Atlantic coast, near the modern town of Padrón. After setting them many trials the ruler of the region, one Queen Lupa, was converted to Christianity and gave them a plot of ground where they interred the Apostle's body.

This brief account cannot record all the medieval documentary and textual references to the reported rediscovery of James's body in the ninth century, nor speculate as to their authenticity. An eleventh century document relates how late in the eighth century a hermit called Pelayo had a vision in which the spot was identified by a star. The local bishop, Theodomir, had ordered a search, the grave of St. James and two of his followers was duly discovered, and a church built over the site. The popular explanation of the name 'compostela' derives from this story, since the word is said to come from 'Campus Stellae' or 'field of the star', but many authorities favour 'compostum' or 'burial ground' as the original meaning.

The fame of the rediscovery quickly spread as rumours of miracles began to circulate. These conveniently coincided with the beginnings of Christian resistance in the kingdoms of northern Spain to the Moorish domination of the rest of the peninsula. When in 844 St James was said to have appeared mounted on a white charger at the head of the victorious Christian forces at the battle of Clavijo, great impetus was given to the determination of the northern kingdoms to win back the territories held by the Moors. St. James became their patron saint and devotion to him was indissolubly linked to the Christian cause.

The consolidation of Christian-held territory in the north made possible access from the rest of Europe to the shrine at Compostela and the traffic of those coming to venerate the Saint's remains increased. In 1078 King Alfonso VI of Castile and León initiated the building of the magnificent cathedral that replaced the former modest church.

The important town of Puente la Reina with its eleventh-century pilgrim bridge.

The Medieval Pilgrimage to Compostela

With the encouragement of the successive kings – Sancho the Great of Navarre (995-1035), Alfonso VI of Castile and León (1065-1109) and Sancho Ramírez of Navarre and Aragon (1076-1094) – the pilgrimage to the shrine of St. James soon came to rival the more famous pilgrimages to Rome and Jerusalem. The Benedictines of Cluny, in particular, were prominent builders of churches and monasteries along the 'Camino Francés' or 'French Road' from the Pyrenees to Compostela. These foundations, and others established by royal patronage or local initiatives, as well as strengthening Christian influence, also provided pilgrims with food, shelter and spiritual care.

Some writers have calculated that the popularity of the pilgrimage to Santiago was such that by the end of the twelfth century, 100,000 pilgrims a year were walking or riding to the shrine. They undertook the arduous journey for a variety of reasons, but which we today could probably place in three simple categories: those of petition (hope of a cure for illness or the granting of some request), penance (to atone for sin, driven by their own consciences or compelled by some authority to go), and thanksgiving.

Pilgrims journeying from all over Europe to what was then considered the edge of the world ('Finisterre' lay only a short distance from Compostela) sought to visit as many other shrines along the way as they could. As the pilgrimage evolved, four routes leading to Spain came to be recognised as major thoroughfares because of the opportunity they afforded of taking in the shrines of other highly venerated saints.

The longest of these was the Via Turonense, which ran from Paris to the Pyrenees, via Tours and the shrine of St. Martin, Poitiers and that of St. Hilaire, Saintes and the tomb of St. Eutrope, and the shrine of St. Seurin at Bordeaux. The Via Lemovicense began at the huge monastery dedicated to St. Mary Magdalene at Vézelay and went by way of Limoges, St. Léonard, and Perigueux. The rock of Le Puy was the starting point of the Via Podensis, which took in the shrine of Ste. Foy at Conques before heading for the Cluniac abbey at Moissac.

The three routes named so far brought pilgrims from northern Europe and Germany into Spain over the heights of Ibañeta to the monastery at Roncesvalles in the western Pyrenees. The Via Tolosana, beginning farther east at Arles and visiting St. Gilles, the shrine of St. Sernin at Toulouse and St.

Interior of the tenth-century church at O Cebreiro.

Waymarking on the Camino.

Guillaume-le-Désert, carried pilgrims from Italy and the Balkans across the Pyrenees via the Somport Pass and the monastery of Santa Cristina. After descending into Aragón, it turned westwards and joined the other route a day's walk west of Pamplona.

These were the routes described in what has been called the 'first travel guide', the fifth book of the *Liber Sancti Jacobi* or *Book of St. James*, better known as the *Codex Calixtinus*. This work was written in the mid-twelfth century by a French monk from Parthenay-le-Vieux called Aimeric Picaud, partly to record his own experience of the journey to Compostela, and partly to assist others attempting the pilgrimage. It describes the regions and shrines along the route, advises the pilgrim on what to see and what to avoid, and discusses – not always kindly – the character and habits of the people through whose lands he will pass.

How widely the information contained in Aimeric Picaud's book was diffused is impossible to tell. Some information about the journey was probably always to be had from the 'confraternities' that were formed in many towns by those who had themselves been to Compostela, and wished to help others enact the pilgrimage. By providing such information the confraternities performed a valuable function: the dangers of the road were many, from poisonous rivers to

The Puerta de Santa María, one of the traditional entries to the city of Burgos.

The pilgrim monument at Santo Domingo de la Calzada, La Rioja.

rapacious innkeepers. There were false pilgrims, too, who might join a solitary traveller, allay his fears and rob or kill him when the chance arose. To minimise such perils, pilgrims tended to travel in groups, setting off together after receiving the blessing of their local priest or bishop. The possessions carried by each would be few: a stout staff, a satchel for food and a gourd or leather bottle for water, and probably, for those who could afford it, a warm cloak and broad-brimmed hat. The scallop shell, at first a token worn on their clothing by pilgrims returning from Compostela, came to be the emblem of the pilgrimage, carried by those seeking to identify themselves as travellers to the shrine of St. James.

Most pilgrims, of course, walked to Compostela, but those who were well-off rode, and took with them their families and retinues of servants. The list of those whose names have a place in history and who are known to have made the pilgrimage – kings and nobles, saints, bishops, and those whose written accounts have come down to us – is very extensive. Among them were Gotescalco, bishop of Le Puy, in 950; the abbot of Montserrat in 959, and a group of pilgrims from the Low Countries in 1065; St. Francis of Assisi, St. Dominic, King Louis VII of France, Matilda, daughter of Henry I of England and widow of the Holy Roman Emperor Henry V, and Catherine of Aragón on her way to her marriage with Henry VIII of England. Her parents, the Catholic monarchs, Ferdinand and Isabella, made the journey in 1496, and finding the pilgrims' hospital in Compostela in disrepair, erected the vast Hostal De Los Reyes Católicos to replace it.

Holy Years

The same Pope Calixtus II, whose encouragement of the pilgrimage led Aimeric Picaud to attach the Pope's name to his guidebook, instituted the Compostellan Holy Year. This occurs whenever the feast of St James – a national holiday in Spain, celebrated on 25 July – falls on a Sunday. There is a pattern to these: they fall every 11, 6, 5 and 6 years and are the cause of great festivity in Santiago de Compostela and along the route. The festivities are all the greater after the 11-year gap, as will be the case in 1993, the next Holy Year. To mark the commencement of the Year, the door of the cathedral of Santiago de Compostela known as the 'Puerta Santa' or Holy Door is opened at midnight on New Year's Eve and remains open for normal access until midnight on the following 31 December.

Astorga: the episcopal palace – never used as such – designed by Antonio Gaudí and today the home of the Museum of the Caminos.

The church of the Virgen del Puente on the 'meseta', Palencia.

The 'Compostela'

Some sort of identification, even a letter of safe conduct, would also have been carried by most genuine pilgrims. As the pilgrimage gained in popularity, attempts were made to control the enormous numbers and protect both pilgrims and local citizens against dishonest travellers. Numerous laws were passed against false pilgrims; others required that pilgrims stay within a few miles of the recognised route.

These regulations were the ancestors of the modern 'compostela' or certificate of pilgrimage granted by the cathedral chapter of Santiago de Compostela to all modern pilgrims who can prove that they have made the journey on foot or by some other accepted means such as bicycle or horseback. This is done by carrying an itinerary card or 'pilgrim passport' which the modern pilgrim can have stamped at churches or town halls along the route. The main stopping places on the card correspond to those that marked the 13 stages or '*etapas*' of the Camino as indicated in Aimeric Picaud's guide. Having obtained his or her compostela, any pilgrim who wants to re-enact a long-standing custom can show it at the front desk of the Hostal de los Reyes Católicos across the square from the cathedral. The building now serves as a luxury hotel, but pilgrims are still given hospitality in the form of a free meal in the hotel kitchen.

'Pilgrim passports' can be obtained from any one of the national associations dedicated to promoting the pilgrimage to Santiago.

Associations of Amigos del Camino de Santiago (Friends of the Road) in Europe

BELGIUM:	Flemish-speaking: J.M. Mondelaers Sint-Andriesabdij-Zevenkerken 8200 Brugge 2
	French-speaking: J.P. Bernard Rue de Marbais 7 6320 Villers la Ville
FRANCE:	Société des Amis de Saint-Jacques de Compostelle Mlle. Jeannine Warcollier 4 Square du Pont de Sèvres 92100 Boulogne sur Seine
	Association Regionale des Amis de St Jacques de Compostelle (Aquitania) Francis Zapata Prieuré de Cayac 257 Cours General de Gaulle 33170 Gradignan
GERMANY:	St. Jakobus Gesellschaft H.K. Bahnen Wilhelmstrasse 50-52 5100 Aachen

H. Wipper
Ziegeleiweg 89
4000 Düsseldorf 13

H. Simon
Melanchtonstr. 24
5000 Köln 80

HOLLAND: Nederlands Genootschap van Sint-Jacob
Frank Claessen
Raaimoeren, 31
NL-4824 KA Breda

ITALY: Centro Italiano di Studi Compostellani
Prof. Paolo Caucci von Saucken.
Via del Verzaro 49
06100 Perugia

SPAIN: Asociación de los Amigos del Camino de Santiago
Coordinador nacional
D. Angel Luis Barreda Ferrer
C/Marqués de Santillana 10-2º
34120 Carrión de los Condes

SWITZERLAND: Asociación Suiza del Camino de Santiago
Joseph Theubet
Lignon 43
1219 Genéve

UNITED KINGDOM: Confraternity of Saint James
Marion Marples
45 Dolben St.
London SE1 OUQ

The Pilgrimage Today

The pilgrimage to Compostela was at its height in the twelfth and thirteenth centuries. War and plague, followed by religious turmoil and further wars, lessened its appeal. Some of the great religious houses and pilgrim hospitals, such as the vast Pyrenean hospice of Santa Cristina and those of Sahagún, declined to the point of ruin. The pilgrim traffic never entirely died out in the intervening centuries, nor did the infrastructure that existed along the Camino de Santiago to help pilgrims on their way.

In the past 10 or 15 years, with the rebirth of interest in the pilgrimage fostered by the 'Amigos del Camino de Santiago' or 'Friends of the Way of St James' in Spain and sister organisations in the other countries of Europe, facilities for pilgrims have increased. Municipal and parochial authorities have augmented the hospitality offered by the many religious communities along the route in making accommodation available to pilgrims. A chain of *refugios* or very basic hostels exists along the Camino for the use of walkers and cyclists. For the most part these facilities are free, but are restricted to

A semi-abandoned village in the mountains of León.

those who can produce a stamped pilgrim itinerary. A donation towards upkeep is appreciated in many *refugios*, but so also is the offer to do some useful task.

Practical advice about long distance walking and cycling is available from many sources. Undertaking the pilgrimage to Compostela, however, is somewhat different from the usual long walk or cycling trip. It is not often recalled that Spain is the most mountainous country in Europe after Switzerland. Both walkers and cyclists need physical resilience, built up through careful preparation to manage a terrain that varies from 1,500 metre passes to arid plateau, and temperatures that in summer can soar to well over 40 degrees. The overall distance from the French border to Santiago is about 800 kilometres, and somewhat farther on the Somport Pass route.

That said, following the actual trajectory of the Camino is no longer difficult, thanks to the systems of yellow arrows initiated by Dr. Elías Valiña in 1984. These were painted by hand on trees, large rocks, poles and buildings to provide simple, instantly recognisable route markers along the whole length of the Camino. They tend to be no more than about 200 metres apart except on the flat tableland of the *meseta* where surfaces on which to paint them are few and far between. On its way through towns the route is usually marked more frequently.

The arrows are renewed annually by volunteers from the provincial associations of '*Amigos*', who well deserve their name for the practical help and advice they can give the modern pilgrim. In addition to the arrows, there are

Give yourself time for reflection and contemplation.

Looking back, at 900 metres, across the plain to Castrojeriz. The whole of the Camino may be traversed by experienced riders on a mountain bike.

other types of waymarking, including stone markers put up by some provincial authorities, and large indicators, of use mainly to motorists, erected by the Council of Europe.

Those undertaking the route in cars should note well the advice on the maps, 'apto para vehiculos' and its opposite, 'no apto...'. The reason part of the route is said to be unsuitable may be because it is really impassable – rock-strewn, excessively rutted by farm machinery or cut by gullies – or because it has been planted over by the local farmers. Cyclists on mountain bikes and those on horseback should be aware of this and exercise judgment. Likewise those in very small cars may prefer to avoid even those sections shown as 'apto'. Exercise common sense, especially when following the route in winter or after heavy rain, and always carry a spare tyre.

The kilometre markings indicated on the maps refer to the current Spanish road system in which roads of different grades can sometimes overlap or change their numbering as a result of successive reconstructions. This can prove a cause of considerable confusion to the traveller.

The Spirit of the Camino

The Camino de Santiago has existed for more than a thousand years. However a person chooses to undertake the pilgrimage to Compostela today – and with whatever spiritual outlook, or with none – he or she will be the poorer without some sense that to be a pilgrim is to carry on a tradition.

As much to honour the millions of fellow pilgrims who have preceded you over the centuries, as to appreciate the experience it offers today, the journey should be undertaken simply and gratefully. Walking or riding to Compostela is an adventure, but one which also leads to interior discovery. It is important not to be hurried, so as to allow time for observing natural features, wildlife and flora, and time for reflection.

A final word as to what makes the pilgrimage to Santiago de Compostela such a special journey: much has been written in all the major European languages to celebrate its blend of historic, artistic and spiritual significance. There are many personal accounts written by pilgrims, many studies on how the same journey was made in ages past. In the end, however great or minimal your preparation, what will make the journey meaningful and memorable is contact

The church of Santa María la Real and ancient Celtic 'pallozas' at O Cebreiro.

'Horreos', or granaries built in the traditional style. The route of the Camino de Santiago through this village in Galicia is indicated by the yellow arrow.

with the people living along the Camino, who view the pilgrimage as a vital expression of Christian faith that has survived the vicissitudes of time, and the pilgrim as precious because he or she is a part of that larger whole.

The pilgrimage is part of these people's lives, as is the custom of showing kindness and hospitality to pilgrims. Remember that these encounters are gifts. There is no way to repay them except to pass them on. Nor is there any way to acknowledge the experience you have gained, except by finding a place for the timeless values of the Camino in the life you return to when your journey is over.

Provincial boundary marker at a meeting point between León and Galicia.

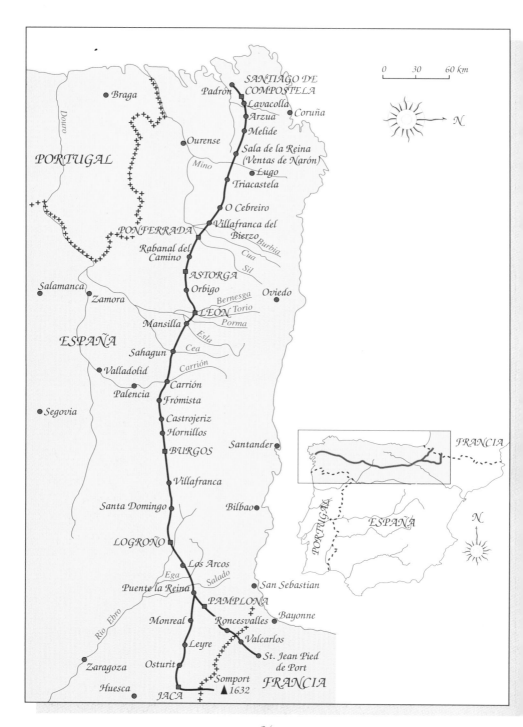

SANTIAGO DE COMPOSTELA

Padrón

Lavacolla

Coruña

Arzua

Melide

Braga

Ourense

Sala de la Reina
(Ventas de Narón)

PORTUGAL

Mino

Lugo

Triacastela

Douro

O Cebreiro

PONFERRADA

Villafranca del
Bierzo

Burbia

Rabanal del
Camino

Cua

Sil

ASTORGA

Salamanca

Orbigo

Oviedo

Zamora

Bernesga

LEON

Torio

Mansilla

Porma

ESPAÑA

Esla

Cea

Sahagun

Valladolid

Carrión

Carrión

Palencia

Frómista

Segovia

Castrojeriz

Hornillos

BURGOS

Santander

Villafranca

Santa Domingo

Bilbao

LOGROÑO

Los Arcos

Ega

Salado

San Sebastian

Puente la Reina

PAMPLONA

Rio Ebro

Monreal

Roncesvalles

Bayonne

Leyre

Valcarlos

Zaragoza

Osturit

St. Jean Pied
de Port

Huesca

Somport
▲1632

JACA

FRANCIA

0   30   60 km

N

FRANCIA

PORTUGAL

ESPAÑA

N

24

LEGEND

▬▬▬ Autopista/Motorway	📋 Estación servicio/Service station
▬ = = Carretera (tunel)/Main road (tunnel)	✚ Cruz roja/Red cross
▬▬ ‑ ‑ Camino de Santiago (tunel)	CS Centro de Salud/Health Centre
‑ ‑ ‑ ‑ Camino secundario/Secondary road	⊕ Farmacia/Chemist, Pharmacy
‑‑·‑·‑ Rutas nuevas/New routes	Ⓐ Alimentación/Food shop
············ Camino de tierra/Unpaved road	✉ Correos/Post office
▥▥▥▥ Camino desap./Road disappeared	Catedral/Cathedral
▬▪▬▪▬ Ferrocarril/Railway	Abadía/Abbey
▬▬▬ Río/River	Ermita/Chapel, Hermitage
▬▬▬ Arroyo/Stream, brook	Iglesia/Church
⋏⋏⋏ Líneas eléctricas/Power lines	+++ Cementerio/Cemetery
+ + + + Frontera internacional/International frontier	† Cruceiro/Cross
‑ + ‑ + Frontera provincial/Provincial boundary	∴ Ruinas/Ruins
AY Ayuntamiento/Town hall	✖ Castillo/Castle
R Refugio/Pilgrim hostel	⊙ Castro/Prehistoric camp
⌣ Lavadero/Laundry	✳ Ruinas arqueológicas/Archaeological remains
IT Información turistica/Tourist office	⬇ Fuente/Fountain, Spring
GC Guardia civil/Civil Guard	⌓ Puente medieval/Medieval bridge
Ⓑ Banco/Bank	🌲 Bosque/Woods, Forests
⊕ Estatua, Monumento/Statue, Monument	🍇 Viñas/Vineyards
○ Pueblo fuera de la ruta/Off route village	– K190 Kilometraje/Kilometre marks
🔍 Ve plano de cuidad/See town plan	▲2923 Montañas, curva de nivel/Mountains, contours lines
	⛺ Camping/Camping

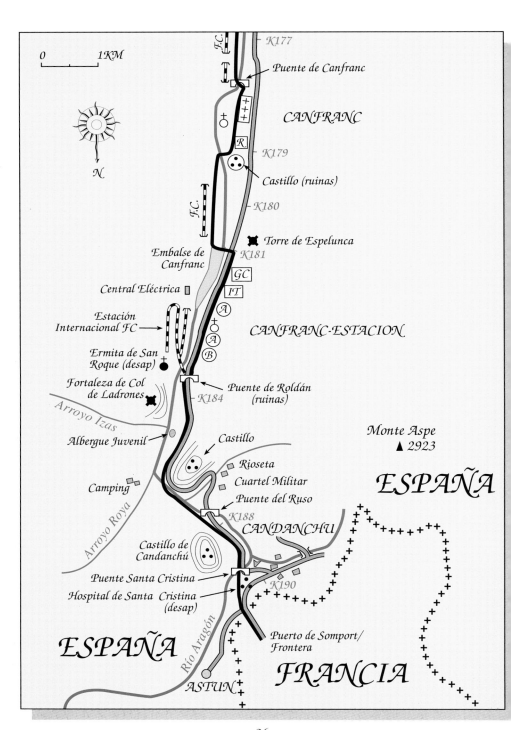

K177

F.C.

Puente de Canfranc

CANFRANC

K179

Castillo (ruinas)

K180

Torre de Espelunca

Embalse de Canfranc

K181

GC

IT

Central Eléctrica

A

Estación Internacional FC

A

B

CANFRANC-ESTACION

Ermita de San Roque (desap)

Fortaleza de Col de Ladrones

Puente de Roldán (ruinas)

K184

Arroyo Izas

Albergue Juvenil

Castillo

Monte Aspe
▲ 2923

Rioseta

Cuartel Militar

ESPAÑA

Camping

Puente del Ruso

Arroyo Roya

K188

CANDANCHU

Castillo de Candanchú

Puente Santa Cristina

Hospital de Santa Cristina (desap)

K190

ESPAÑA

Río Aragón

Puerto de Somport/ Frontera

FRANCIA

ASTUN

0   1KM

N

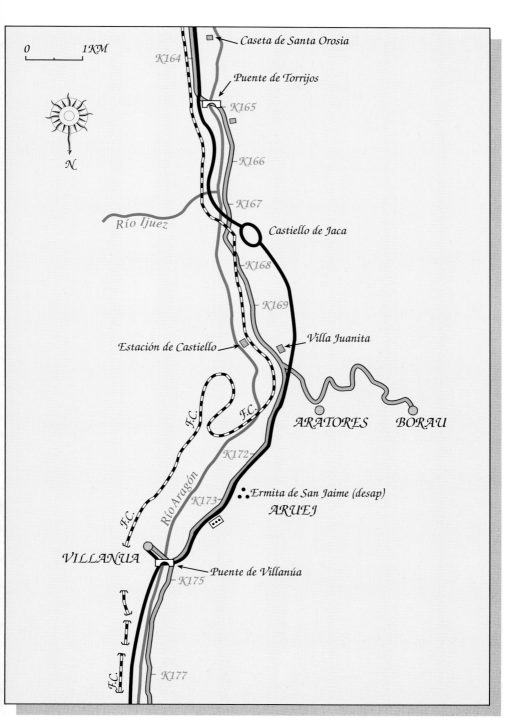

0   1KM

Caseta de Santa Orosia

K164

Puente de Torrijos

K165

K166

K167

Río Ijuez

Castiello de Jaca

K168

K169

Estación de Castiello

Villa Juanita

F.C.

F.C.

ARATORES

BORAU

K172

Río Aragón

K173

Ermita de San Jaime (desap)

ARUEJ

F.C.

VILLANÚA

Puente de Villanúa

K175

F.C.

K177

N

27

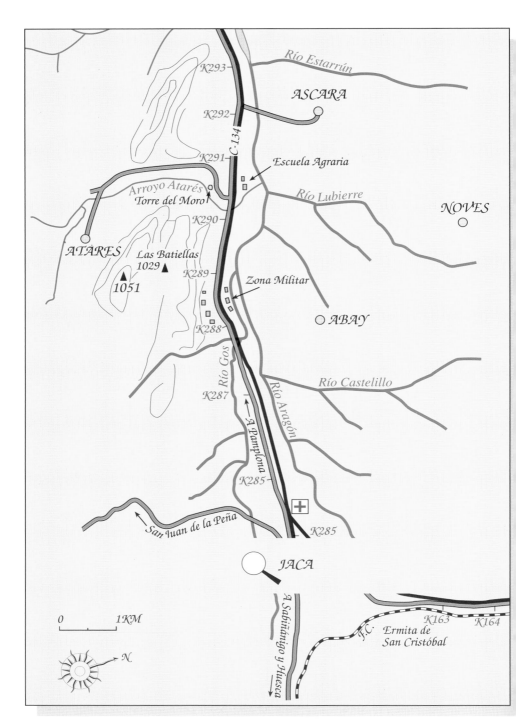

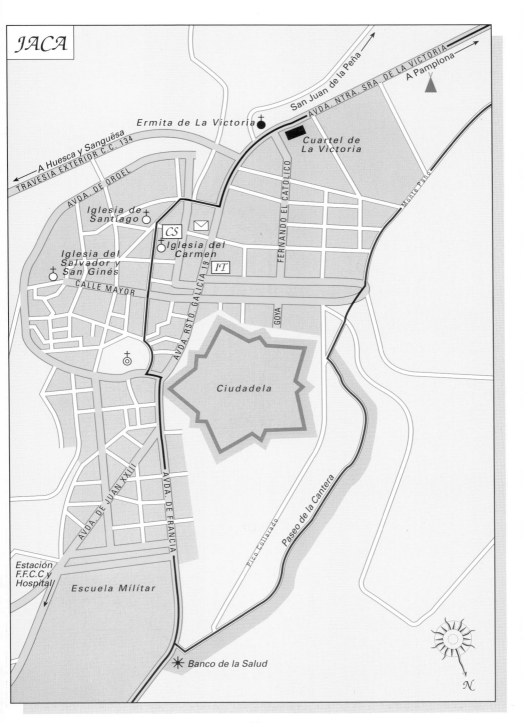

JACA

A Huesca y Sanguësa
TRAVESIA EXTERIOR C.C. 134

San Juan de la Peña

AVDA. NTRA. SRA. DE LA VICTORIA

A Pamplona

Ermita de La Victoria

Cuartel de La Victoria

AVDA. DE OROEL

FERNANDO EL CATÓLICO

Monte Pano

Iglesia de Santiago

CS

Iglesia del Carmen

Iglesia del Salvador y San Ginés

IT

CALLE MAYOR

AVDA. RSTO. GALICIA 19

GOYA

Ciudadela

AVDA. DE FRANCIA

AVDA. DE JUAN XXII

Paseo de la Cantera

Pico Collarado

Estación
F.F.C.C y
Hospital

Escuela Mílitar

Banco de la Salud

N

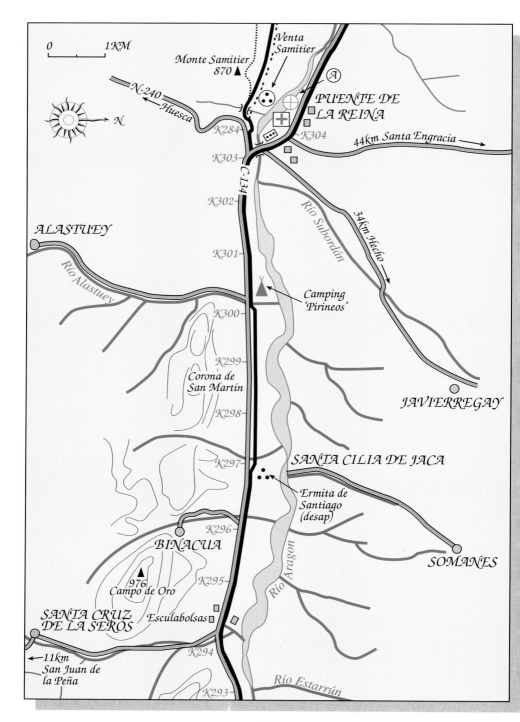

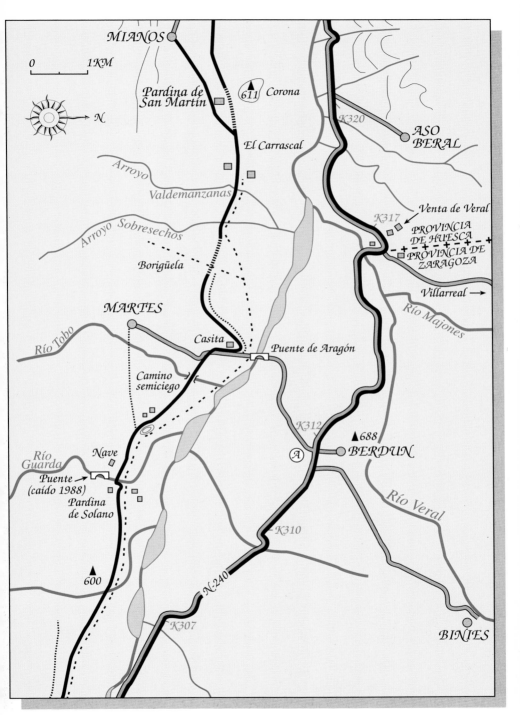

MIANOS

0 1KM

N

Pardina de
San Martín

▲611 Corona

El Carrascal

Arroyo

Valdemanzanas

Arroyo Sobresechos

BoriGüela

MARTES

Río Tobo

Casita

Camino
semiciego

Río
Guarda

Nave

Puente →
(caído 1988)
Pardina
de Solano

▲
600

K320

ASO
BERAL

Venta de Veral

K317

PROVINCIA
DE HUESCA
+ — + — + —
PROVINCIA DE
ZARAGOZA

Villarreal →

Río Majones

Puente de Aragón

K312

Ⓐ

▲688

BERDÚN

Río Veral

K310

N-240

K307

BINIES

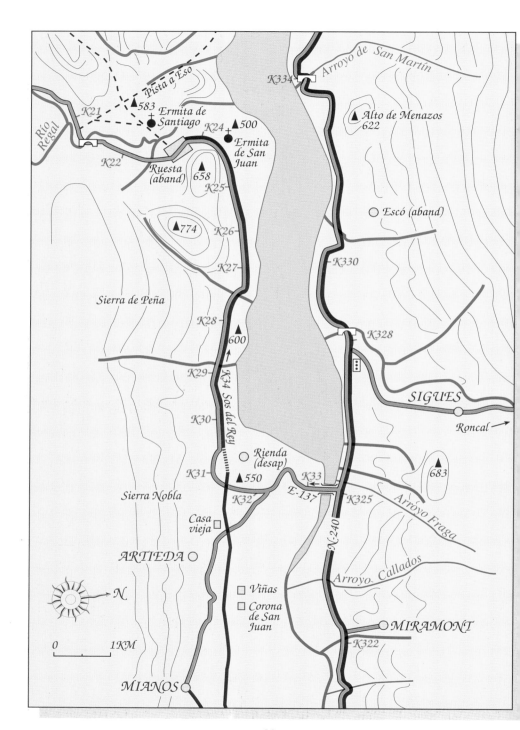

Arroyo de San Martín

K334

Pista a Eso

K21

▲583
+ Ermita de Santiago

▲ Alto de Menazos
622

Río Regal

K24 ▲500
+ Ermita de San Juan

K22

Ruesta (aband)

▲658

K25

○ Escó (aband)

▲774

K26

K27

K330

Sierra de Peña

K28

▲600

K29

K34 Sos del Rey

☐ K328

SIGUES

K30

Roncal →

Rienda (desap)

K31

▲550

K33

▲683

Sierra Nobla

K32

E-137

K325

Arroyo Fraga

Casa vieja ☐

N-240

ARTIEDA ○

Arroyo Callados

→ N

☐ Viñas

☐ Corona de San Juan

○ MIRAMONT

0   1KM

K322

MIANOS ○

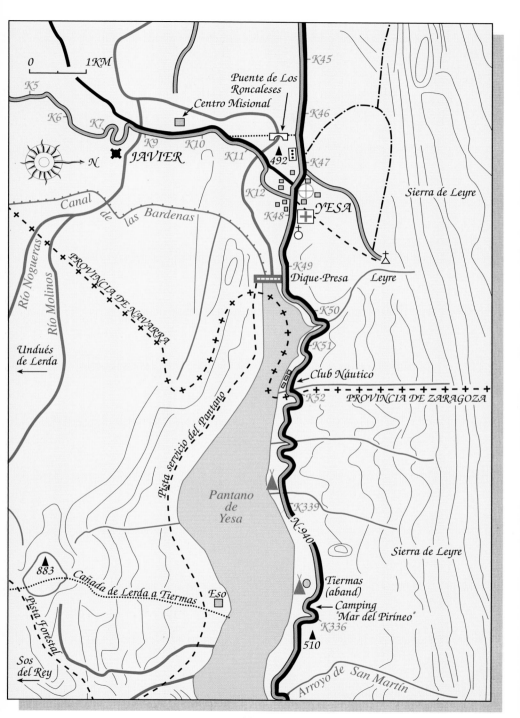

33

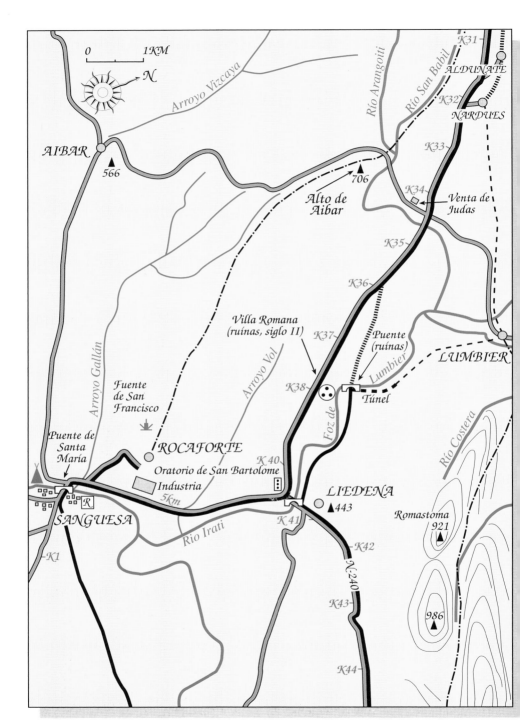

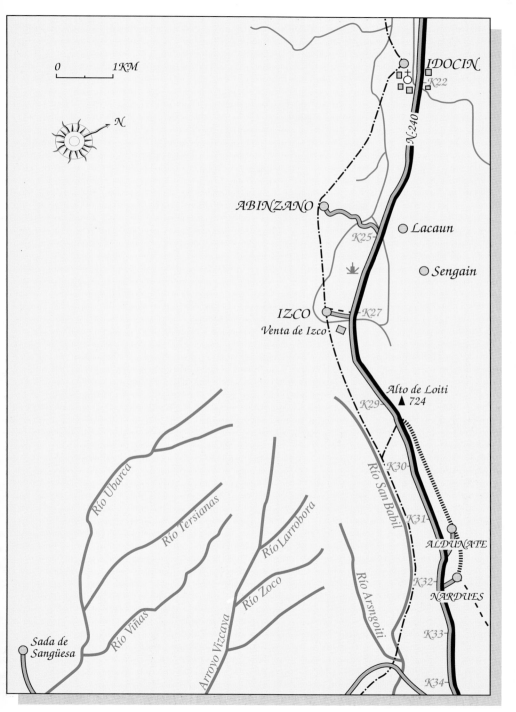

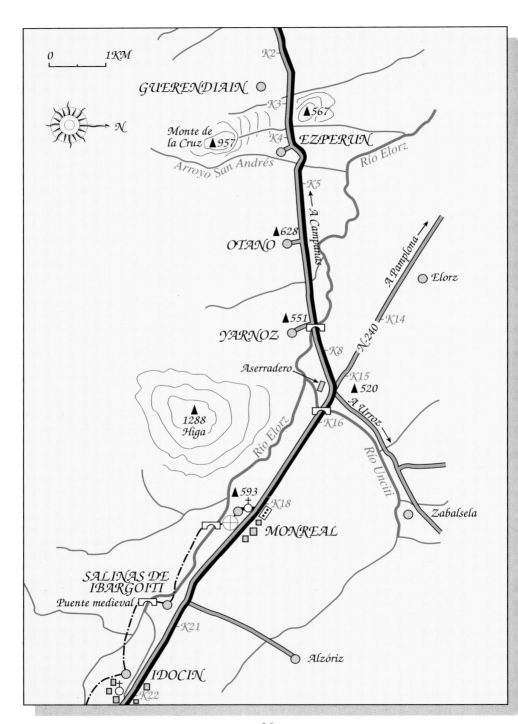

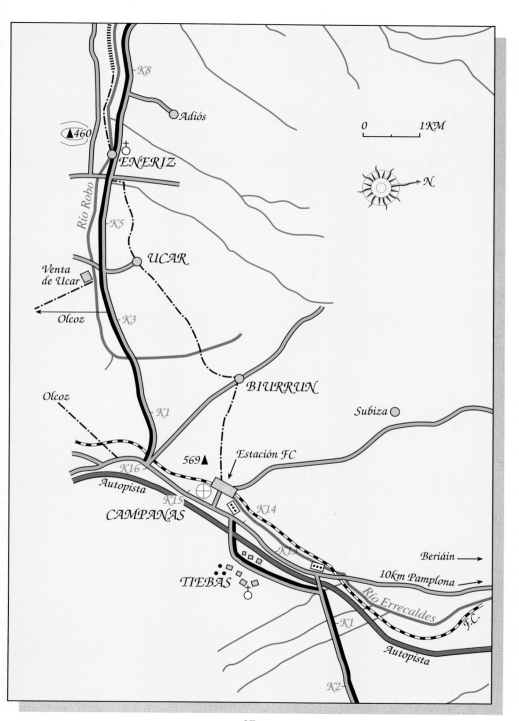

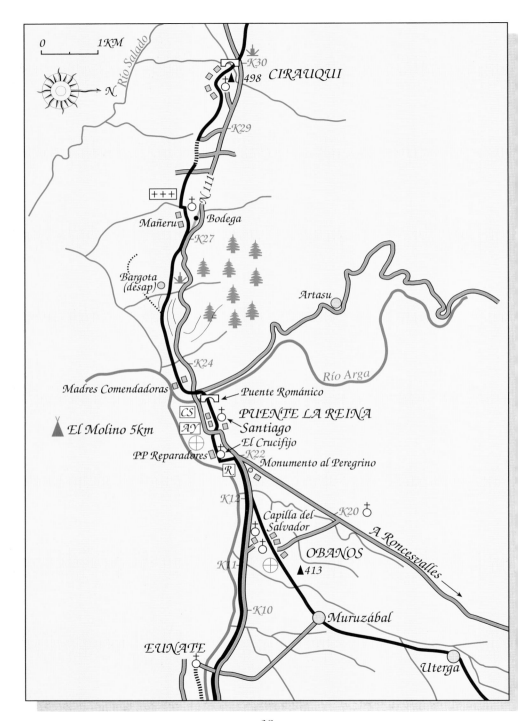

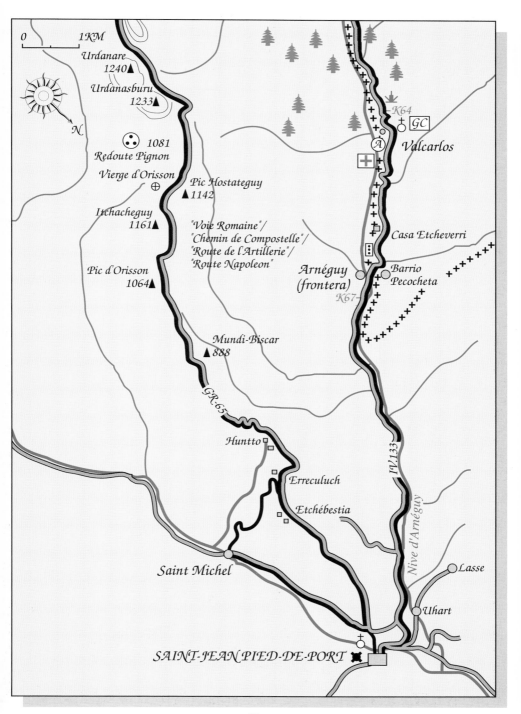

0 · · · · 1KM

N

Urdanare
1240▲

Urdanasburu
1233▲

1081
Redoute Pignon

Vierge d'Orisson

Pic Hostateguy
▲1142

Itchacheguy
1161▲

"Voie Romaine"/
"Chemin de Compostelle"/
"Route de l'Artillerie"/
"Route Napoleon"

Pic d'Orisson
1064▲

K64

GC

Valcarlos

Casa Etcheverri

Arnéguy
(frontera)

Barrio
Pecocheta

K67

Mundi-Biscar
▲888

GR-65

Huntto

Erreculuch

Etchébestia

IV.133

Nive d'Arnéguy

Saint Michel

Lasse

Uhart

SAINT-JEAN·PIED-DE-PORT

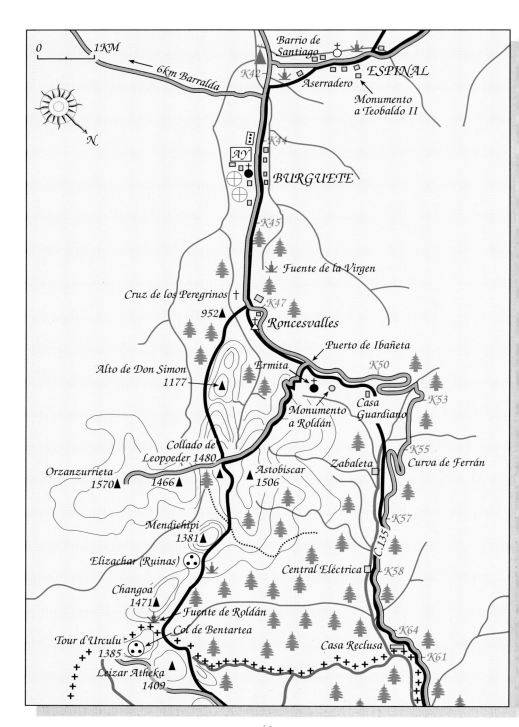

0   1KM

N

6km Barralda

Barrio de Santiago

ESPINAL

K42

Aserradero

Monumento a Teobaldo II

K44

AY

BURGUETE

K45

Fuente de la Virgen

Cruz de los Peregrinos

952▲

K47

Roncesvalles

Puerto de Ibañeta

K50

Alto de Don Simon 1177

Ermita

K53

Monumento a Roldán

Casa Guardiano

Collado de Leopoeder 1480

Zabaleta

K55

Curva de Ferrán

Orzanzurrieta 1570▲

1466▲

Astobiscar 1506

Mendichipi 1381▲

C.135

K57

Elizachar (Ruinas)

Central Eléctrica

K58

Changoa 1471▲

Fuente de Roldán

Tour d'Urculu 1385

Col de Bentartea

Casa Reclusa

K64

K61

Leizar Atheka 1409

40

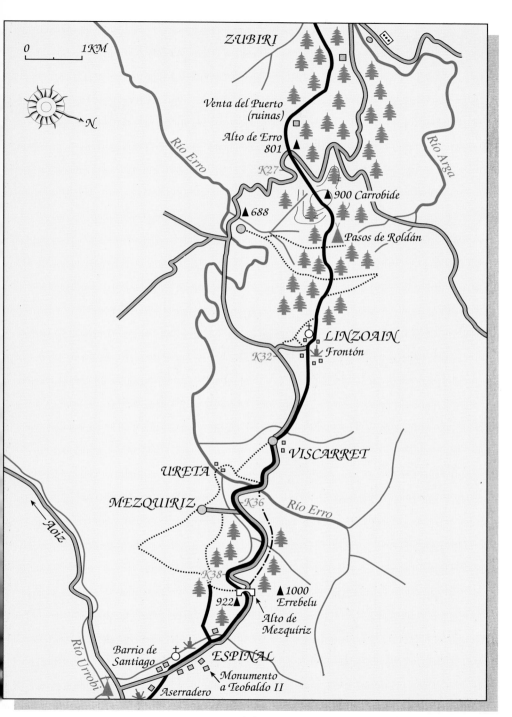

ZUBIRI

Venta del Puerto
(ruinas)

Alto de Erro
801

K27

Río Erro

Río Arga

▲900 Carrobide

▲688

Pasos de Roldán

✝
○ LINZOAIN
Frontón

K32

VISCARRET

URETA

MEZQUIRIZ

K36   Río Erro

Aoiz

K38

▲1000
Errebelu

922▲

Alto de
Mezquíriz

Río Urrobi

Barrio de
Santiago

✝
○ ESPINAL

Monumento
a Teobaldo II

Aserradero

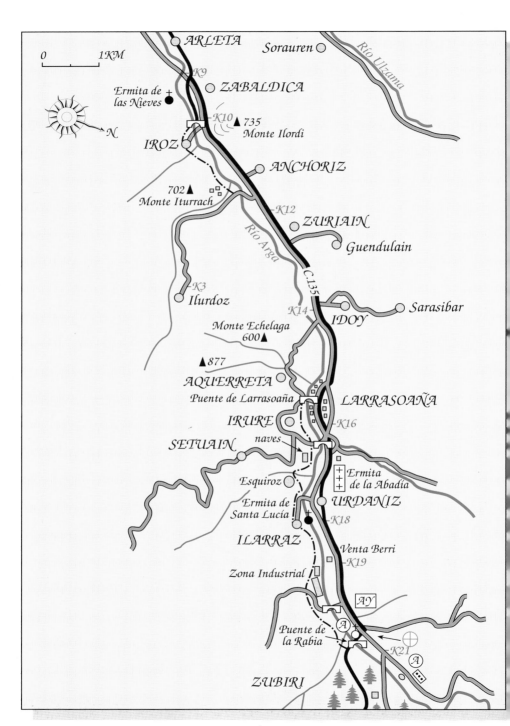

ARLETA · Sorauren · Río Ulzama

0   1KM

K9

ZABALDICA

Ermita de las Nieves

K10 ▲ 735 Monte Ilordi

IROZ

N

ANCHORIZ

702 ▲ Monte Iturrach

K12

ZURIAIN

Guendulain

Río Arga

C.135

K3 Ilurdoz

K14

IDOY Sarasibar

Monte Echelaga 600 ▲

▲ 877

AQUERRETA

Puente de Larrasoaña

LARRASOAÑA

IRURE

K16

SETUAIN naves

Ermita de la Abadía

Esquiroz

URDANIZ

Ermita de Santa Lucía

K18

ILARRAZ

Venta Berri

K19

Zona Industrial

AY

A

Puente de la Rabia

K21

A

ZUBIRI

42

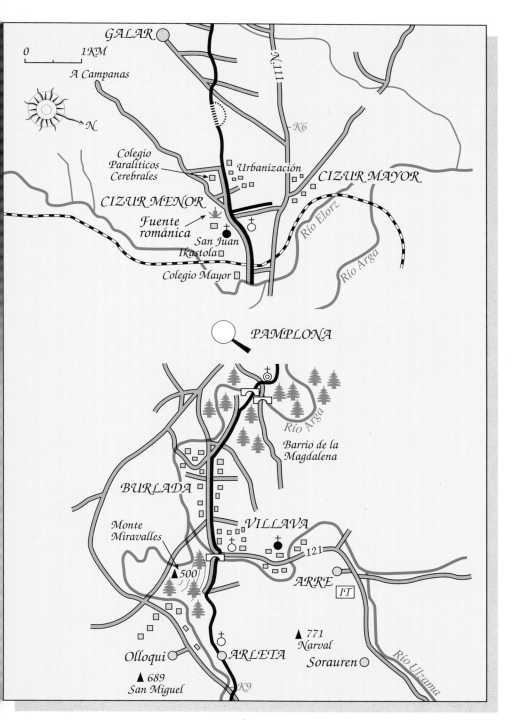

GALAR

A Campanas

N

0   1KM

N-111

K6

Colegio
Paralíticos
Cerebrales

Urbanización

CIZUR MAYOR

CIZUR MENOR

Fuente
románica

Río Elorz

San Juan
Ikastola

Río Arga

Colegio Mayor

PAMPLONA

Río Arga

Barrio de la
Magdalena

BURLADA

VILLAVA

Monte
Miravalles

121

▲500

ARRE

I·T

Olloqui

ARLETA

▲771
Narval

Sorauren

Río Ulzama

▲689
San Miguel

K9

43

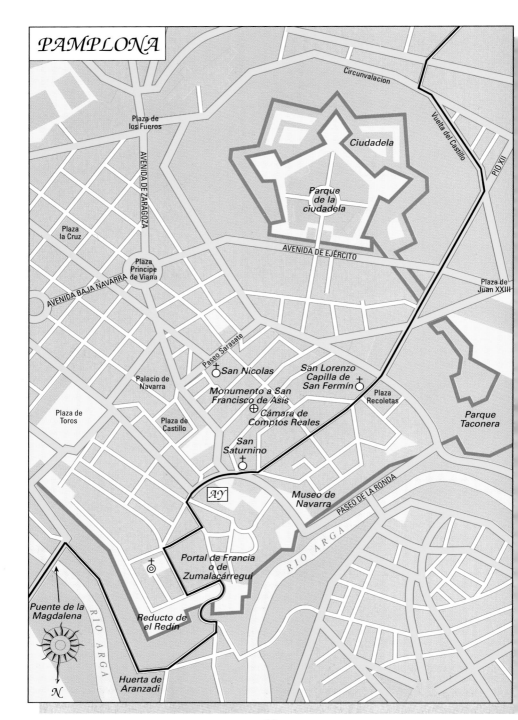

PAMPLONA

Plaza de los Fueros

Circunvalacion

Vuelta del Castillo

Ciudadela

RIO XII

AVENIDA DE ZARAGOZA

Parque de la ciudadela

Plaza la Cruz

Plaza Principe de Viana

AVENIDA DE EJÉRCITO

AVENIDA BAJA NAVARRA

Plaza de Juan XXIII

Paseo Sarasate

San Nicolas

San Lorenzo Capilla de San Fermín

Plaza Recoletas

Palacio de Navarra

Monumento a San Francisco de Asís

Parque Taconera

Plaza de Toros

Cámara de Comptos Reales

Plaza de Castillo

San Saturnino

AY

Museo de Navarra

PASEO DE LA RONDA

RIO ARGA

Portal de Francia o de Zumalacárregui

Puente de la Magdalena

RIO ARGA

Reducto de el Redín

N

Huerta de Aranzadi

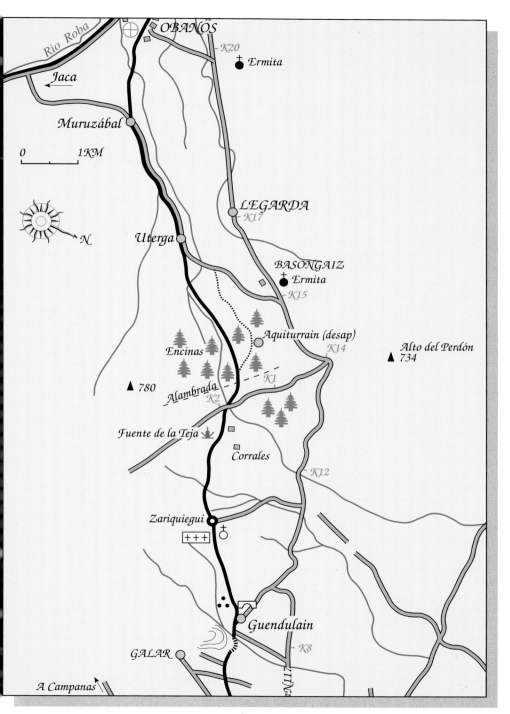

Río Roba

OBANOS
K20
✝ Ermita

Jaca

Muruzábal

0   1KM

N

LEGARDA
K17

Uterga

BASONGAIZ
✝ Ermita
K15

▲ 780

Encinas

Aquiturrain (desap)
K14

Alto del Perdón
▲ 734

Alambrada
K1
K2

Fuente de la Teja

Corrales

K12

Zariquiegui
+++ ✝
○

Guendulain
K8

GALAR

A Campanas

45

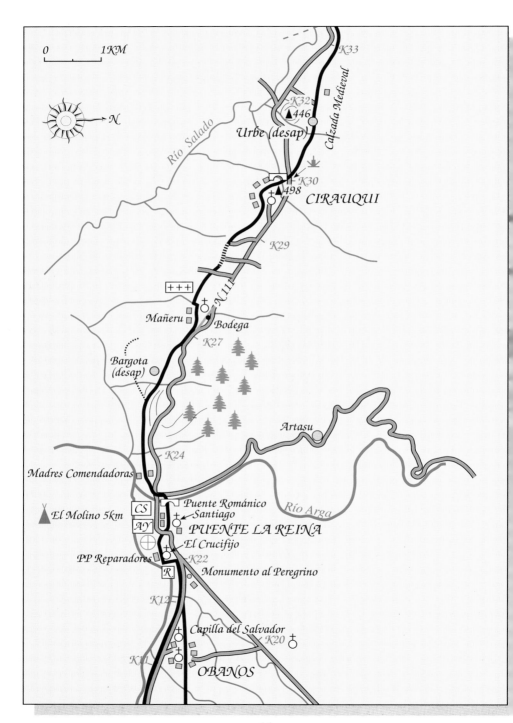

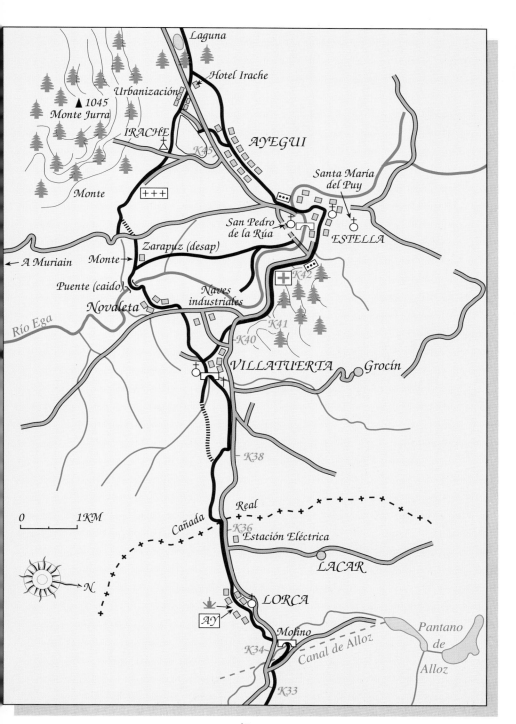

Laguna

Hotel Irache

Urbanización

▲ 1045
Monte Jurra

IRACHE

AYEGUI

K45

Santa María
del Puy

Monte

+ + +

San Pedro
de la Rúa

ESTELLA

Zarapuz (desap)

A Muriain

Monte

K42

Puente (caido)

Naves
industriales

Novaleta

Río Ega

K41

K40

VILLATUERTA

Grocín

K38

Real

0   1KM

Cañada

K36

Estación Eléctrica

N

LACAR

LORCA

AY

Molino

Pantano
de

K34

Canal de Alloz

Alloz

K33

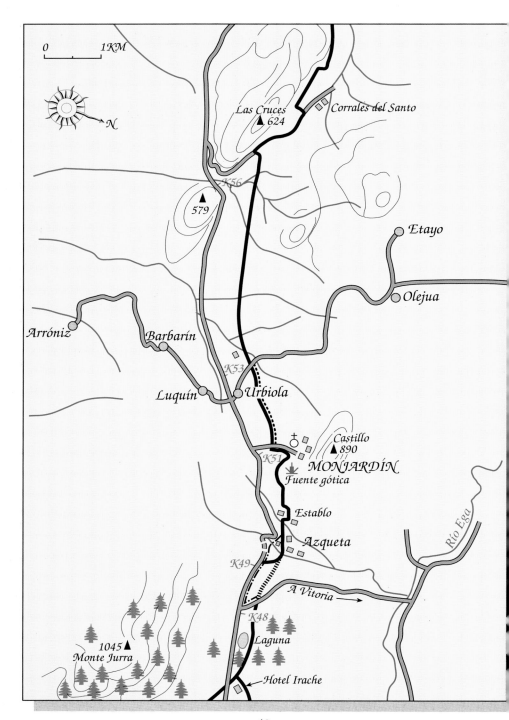

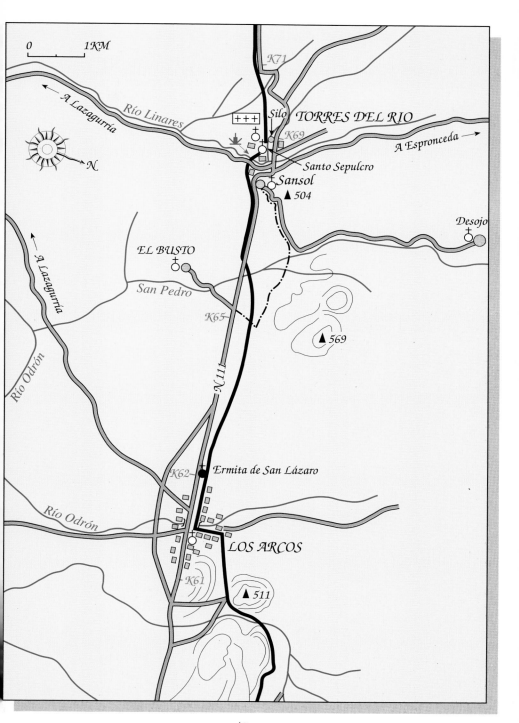

0   1KM

A Lazagurría

Río Linares

Silo

+ + +

TORRES DEL RIO

K71

K69

A Espronceda

N

Santo Sepulcro

Sansol

▲ 504

Desojo

A Lazagurría

EL BUSTO

San Pedro

K65

▲ 569

N111

Río Odrón

Río Odrón

K62

Ermita de San Lázaro

LOS ARCOS

K61

▲ 511

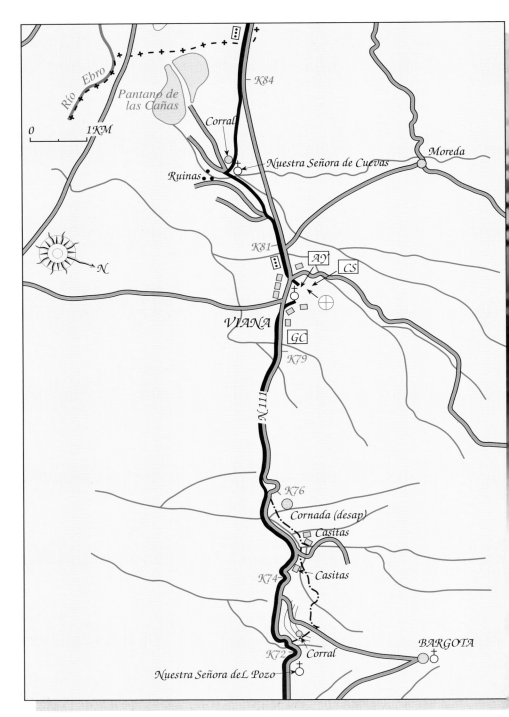

Río Ebro

Pantano de
las Cañas

Corral

Nuestra Señora de Cuevas

Ruinas

Moreda

K84

0   1KM

N

K81

AY

CS

VIANA

GC

K79

N111

K76

Cornada (desap)

Casitas

Casitas

K74

Corral

BARGOTA

K72

Nuestra Señora deL Pozo

50

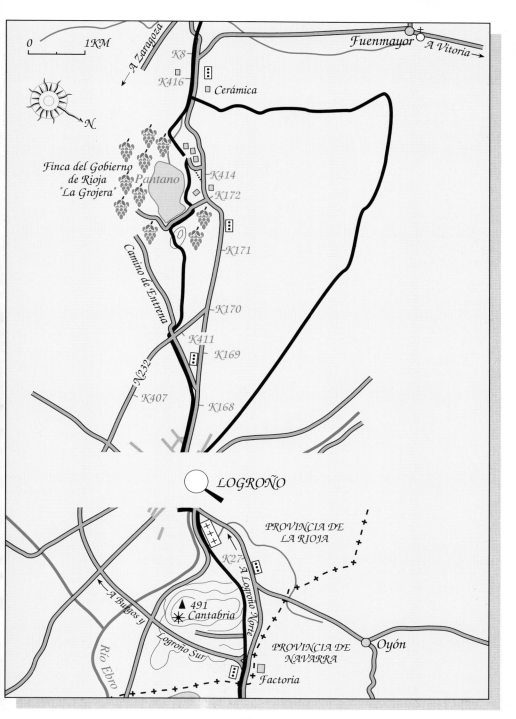

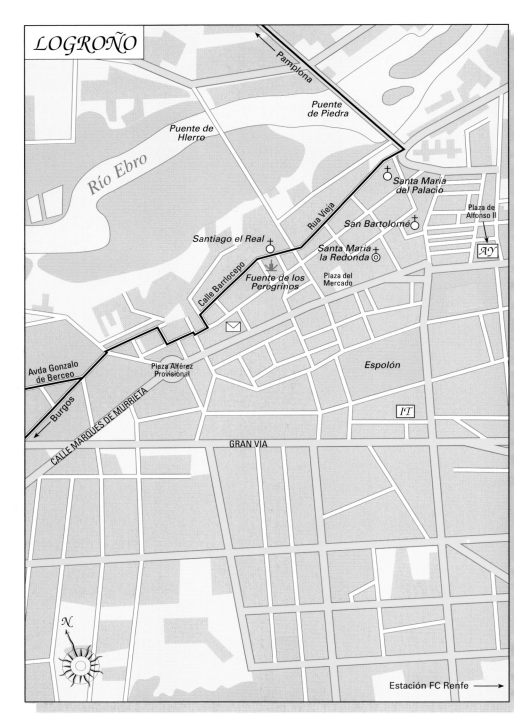

LOGROÑO

Pamplona

Puente de Piedra

Puente de Hlerro

Río Ebro

Santa María del Palacio

Plaza de Alfonso II

Rua Vieja

San Bartolomé

Santiago el Real

Santa María la Redonda

Calle Barriocepo

Fuente de los Peregrinos

Plaza del Mercado

AY

Avda Gonzalo de Berceo

Plaza Alférez Provisional

Espolón

Burgos

CALLE MARQUÉS DE MURRIETA

IT

GRAN VIA

N

Estación FC Renfe ⟶

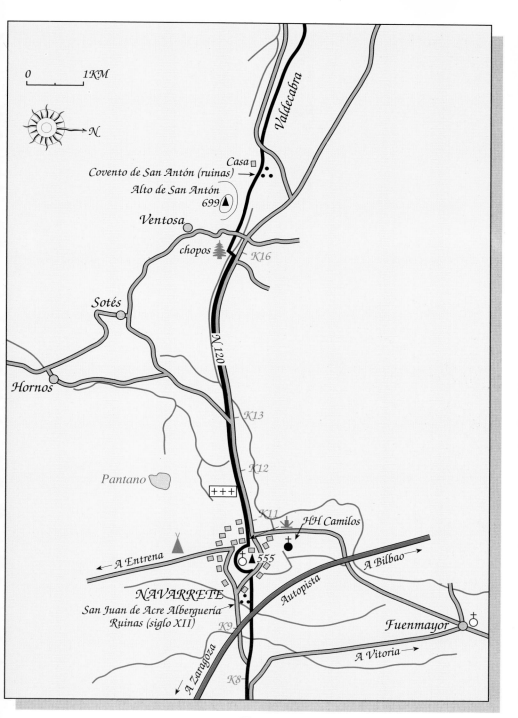

Covento de San Antón (ruinas) →
Alto de San Antón
699 ▲

Casa

Valdecabra

Ventosa

chopos

K16

Sotés

N 120

Hornos

K13

K12

Pantano

+++

K11

HH Camilos

A Entrena

555

Autopista

A Bilbao

NAVARRETE
San Juan de Acre Alberguería
Ruinas (siglo XII)

K9

A Vitoria →

Fuenmayor

A Zaragoza

K8

0   1KM

N

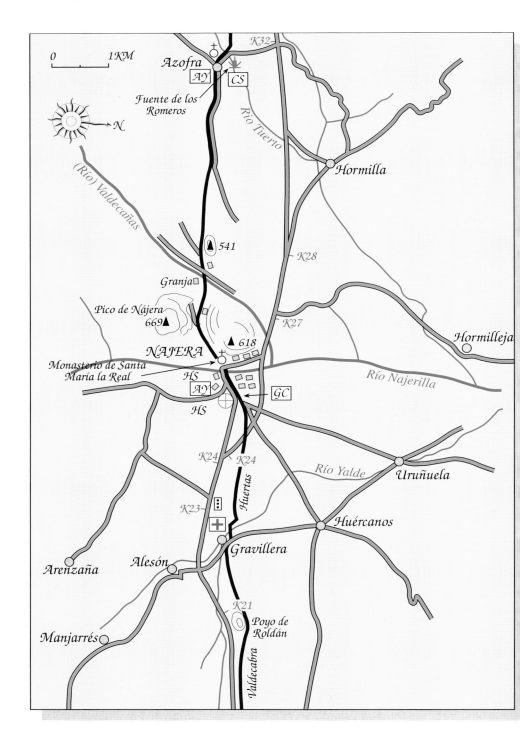

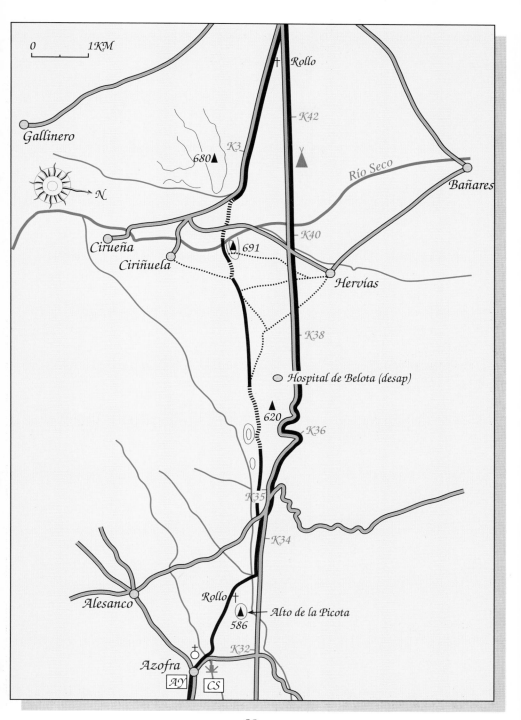

0   1KM

Gallinero

✝ Rollo

— K42

K3
680▲

Río Seco

Bañares

N

Cirueña

Ciriñuela

▲ 691

— K40

Hervías

— K38

Hospital de Belota (desap)

▲
620   — K36

— K35

— K34

Alesanco

Rollo ✝

▲ ← Alto de la Picota
586

— K32

Azofra

AY   CS

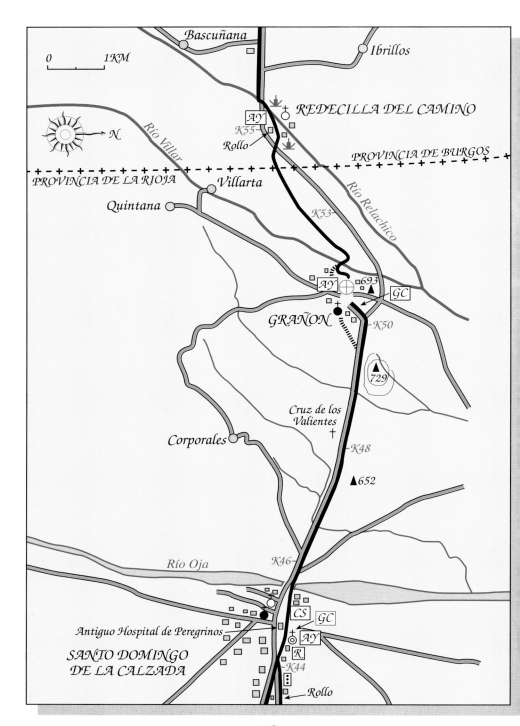

Bascuñana

Ibrillos

0   1KM

N

Río Villar

REDECILLA DEL CAMINO

AY
K55
Rollo

PROVINCIA DE BURGOS

PROVINCIA DE LA RIOJA

Villarta

Río Relachico

Quintana

K53

AY   693
GC

GRAÑON

K50

729

Cruz de los
Valientes

Corporales

K48

652

Río Oja

K46

CS   GC

Antiguo Hospital de Peregrinos

AY
R

SANTO DOMINGO
DE LA CALZADA

K44

Rollo

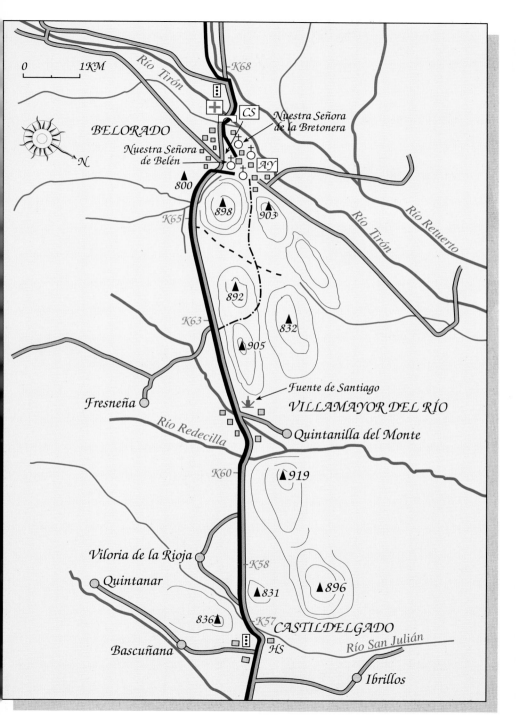

0   1KM

Río Tirón   K68

BELORADO

CS

Nuestra Señora
de la Bretonera

N

Nuestra Señora
de Belén

AY

800

898   903

K65

Río Tirón   Río Retuerto

892

K63

832

905

Fuente de Santiago

Fresneña   VILLAMAYOR DEL RÍO

Río Redecilla   Quintanilla del Monte

K60

919

Viloria de la Rioja

Quintanar   K58

831   896

836

K57   CASTILDELGADO

Bascuñana   HS

Río San Julián

Ibrillos

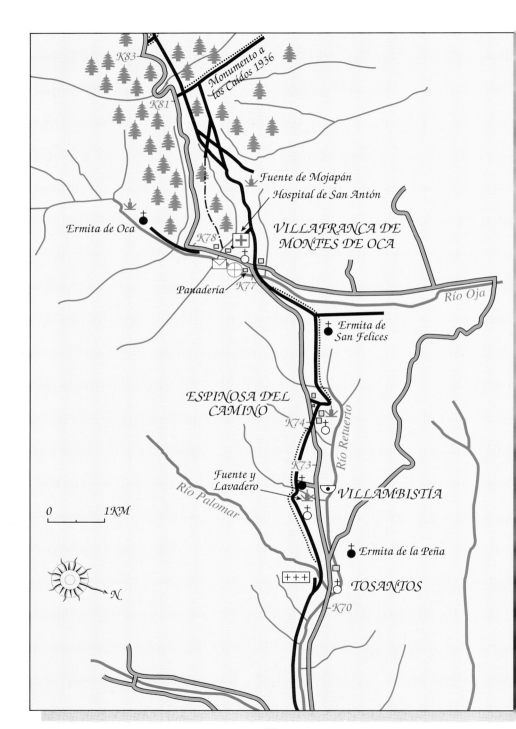

K83

K81

Monumento a
los Caídos 1936

Fuente de Mojapán

Hospital de San Antón

Ermita de Oca

VILLAFRANCA DE
MONTES DE OCA

K78

Panadería

K77

Río Oja

Ermita de
San Felices

ESPINOSA DEL
CAMINO

K74

Río Retuerto

K73

Fuente y
Lavadero

Río Palomar

VILLAMBISTÍA

0   1KM

Ermita de la Peña

N

+ + +

TOSANTOS

K70

58

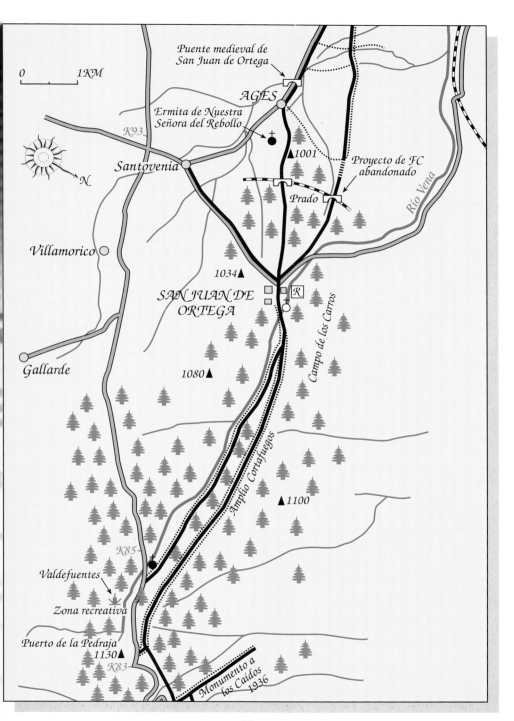

Puente medieval de
San Juan de Ortega

AGES

Ermita de Nuestra
Señora del Rebollo

K93

Santovenia

Proyecto de FC
abandonado

▲1001

Prado

Río Vena

Villamorico

1034▲

SAN JUAN DE
ORTEGA

R

Campo de los Carros

Gallarde

1080 ▲

Amplio Cortafuegos

▲1100

K85

Valdefuentes

Zona recreativa

Puerto de la Pedraja
1130▲

K83

Monumento a
los Caídos
1936

0   1KM

N

59

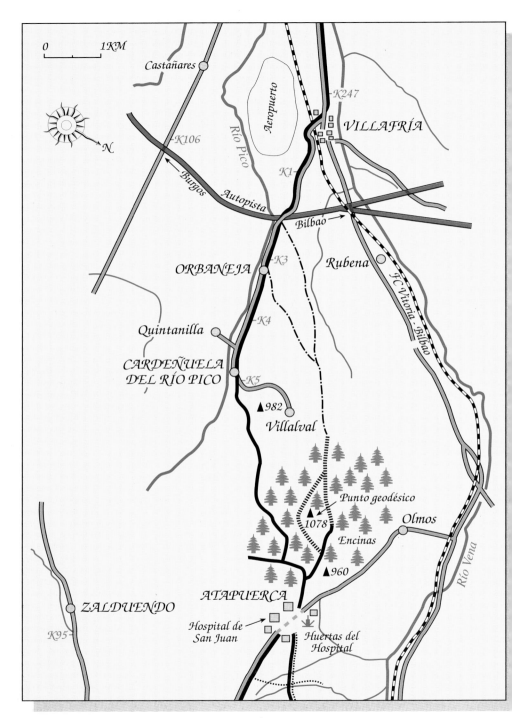

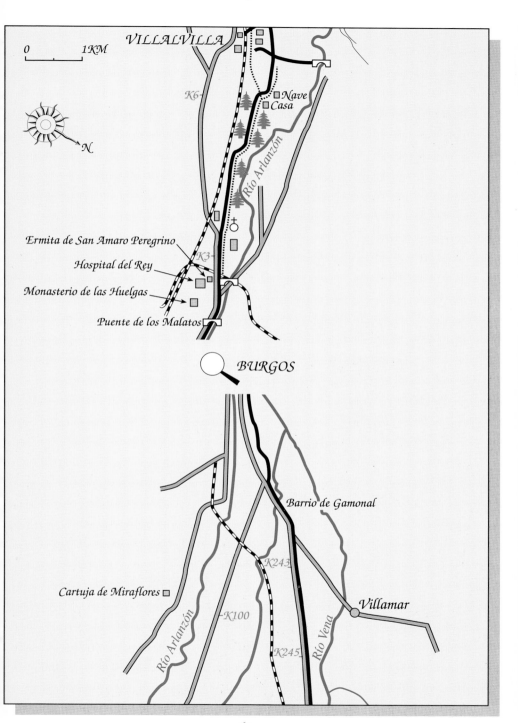

VILLALVILLA

0   1KM

N

K6

Nave
Casa

Río Arlanzón

Ermita de San Amaro Peregrino
K3
Hospital del Rey
Monasterio de las Huelgas
Puente de los Malatos

BURGOS

Barrio de Gamonal

K243

Cartuja de Miraflores

K100

Villamar

Río Arlanzón

K245

Río Vena

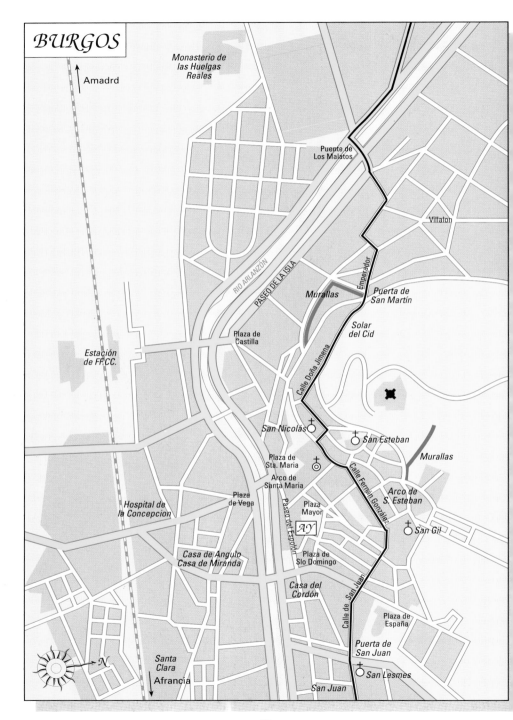

BURGOS

Amadrd

Monasterio de
las Huelgas
Reales

Puente de
Los Malatos

Villaton

RIO ARLANZÓN

PASEO DE LA ISLA

Emperador

Murallas

Puerta de
San Martín

Solar
del Cid

Plaza de
Castilla

Calle Doña Jimena

Estación
de FF.CC.

San Nicolás

San Esteban

Murallas

Plaza de
Sta. Maria

Arco de
Santa Maria

Arco de
S. Esteban

Plaza
de Vega

Calle Fernán González

Hospital de
la Concepcion

Plaza
Mayor

AY

San Gil

Paseo del Espolón

Casa de Angulo
Casa de Miranda

Plaza de
Sto Domingo

Casa del
Cordón

Calle de San Juan

Plaza de
España

Santa
Clara

Afrancia

Puerta de
San Juan

San Lesmes

San Juan

N

62

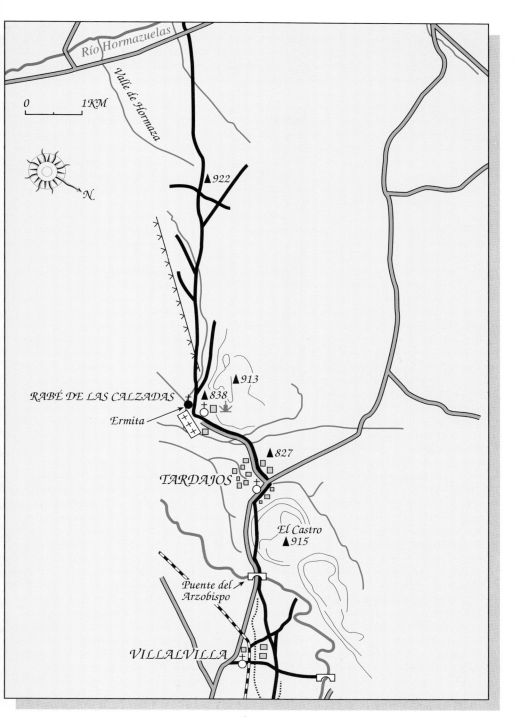

Río Hormazuelas

Valle de Hormaza

0 1KM

N

▲922

▲913

RABÉ DE LAS CALZADAS

▲838

Ermita

▲827

TARDAJOS

El Castro
▲915

Puente del
Arzobispo

VILLALVILLA

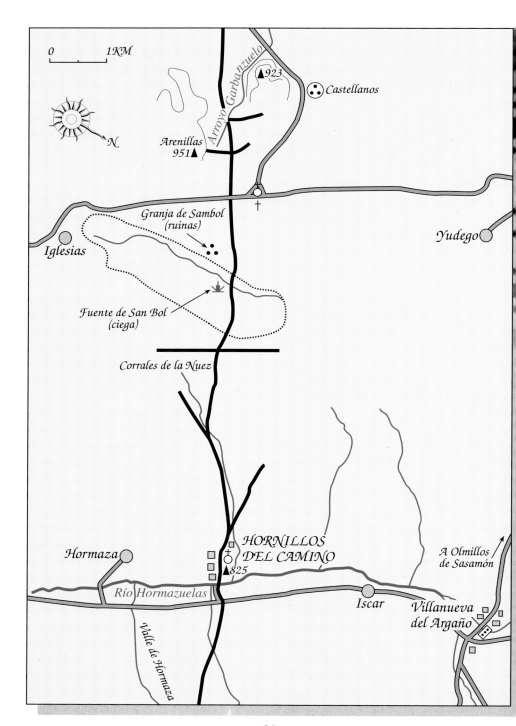

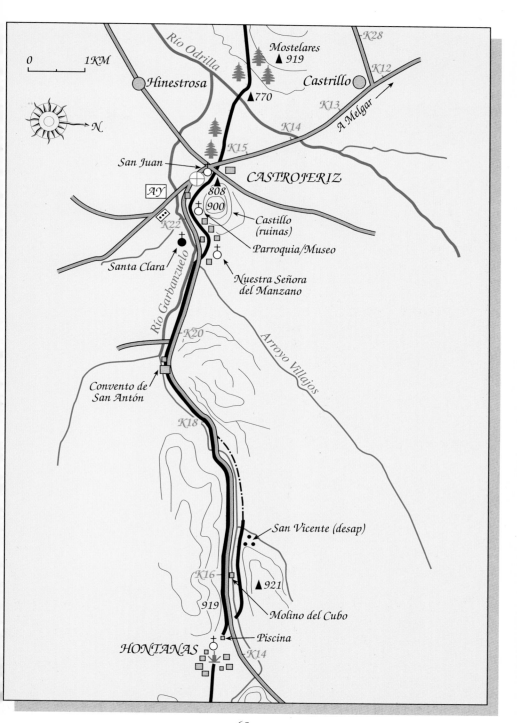

0   1KM

N

Río Odrilla

Hinestrosa

Mostelares
▲ 919

Castrillo

K28

K12

K13

▲770

A Melgar

K14

K15

San Juan

AY

CASTROJERIZ

▲
808
✝ 900

Castillo
(ruinas)

K22

Parroquia/Museo

Santa Clara

✝ Nuestra Señora
del Manzano

Río Garbanzuelo

K20

Arroyo Villajos

Convento de
San Antón

K18

San Vicente (desap)

K16

▲921

919

Molino del Cubo

✝ Piscina

HONTANAS

K14

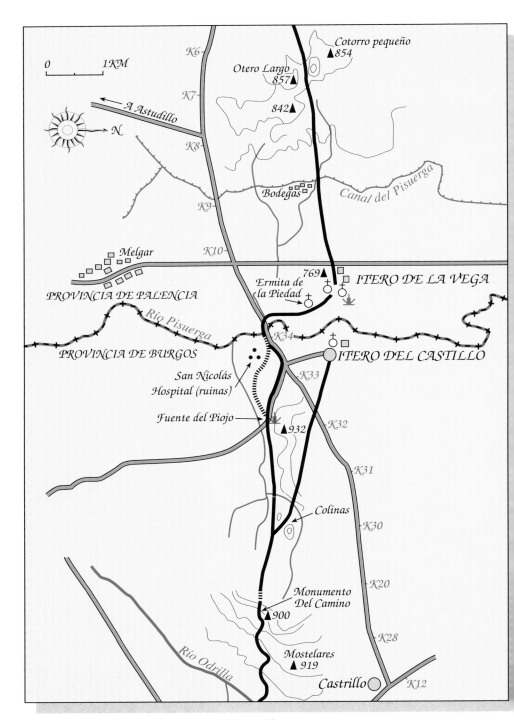

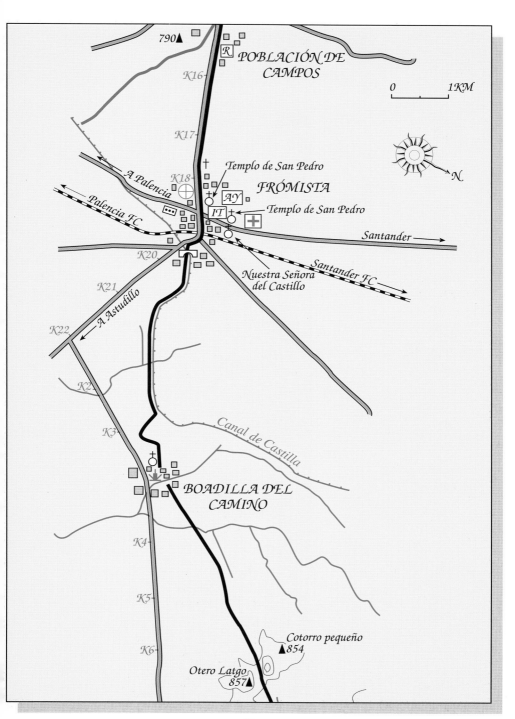

790▲

R POBLACIÓN DE
   CAMPOS

0   1KM

K16

K17

N

† Templo de San Pedro
A Palencia
K18
†
AY FRÓMISTA
Palencia FC
IT † Templo de San Pedro
✚

Santander →

K20
Santander FC
Nuestra Señora
del Castillo

K21

A Astudillo

K22

K2

Canal de Castilla

K3

†
✚ BOADILLA DEL
   CAMINO

K4

K5

K6

Cotorro pequeño
▲854

Otero Latgo
857▲

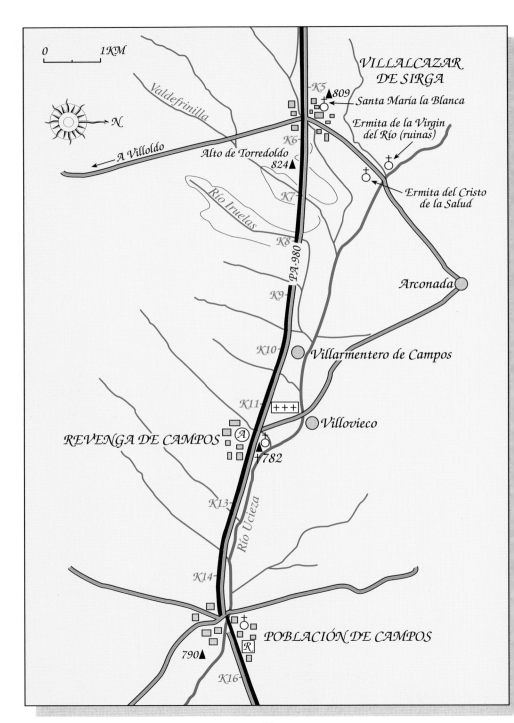

0   1KM

N

Valdefrinilla

VILLALCAZAR
DE SIRGA

K5
▲809
Santa María la Blanca

Ermita de la Virgin
del Río (ruinas)

A Villoldo

Alto de Torredoldo

K6

824▲

Ermita del Cristo
de la Salud

Río Iruelas

K7

K8

PA-980

Arconada

K9

K10

Villarmentero de Campos

K11

+ + +

REVENGA DE CAMPOS

Ⓐ

Villovieco

+782

K13

Río Ucieza

K14

POBLACIÓN DE CAMPOS

790▲

Ⓡ

K16

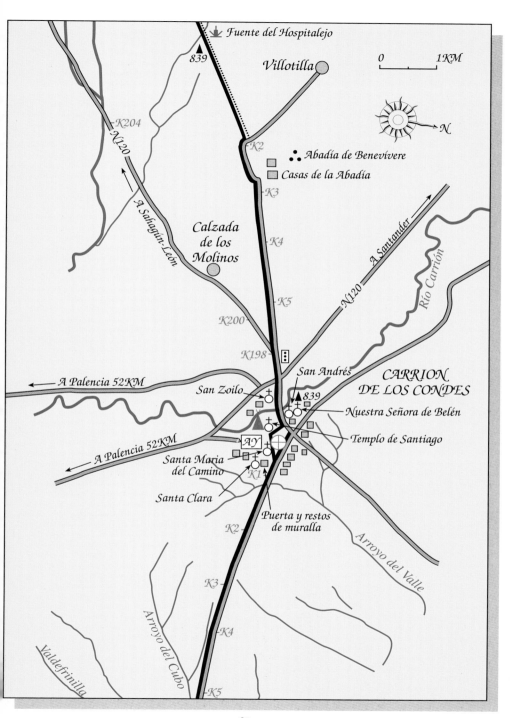

Fuente del Hospitalejo

▲ 839

Villotilla

0   1KM

K204

N120

K2

∴ Abadía de Benevívere
☐ Casas de la Abadía

A Sahagún-León

K3

Calzada
de los
Molinos

K4

A Santander

N120

Río Carrión

K5

K200

K198

CARRION
DE LOS CONDES

A Palencia 52KM

San Andrés

San Zoilo

▲ 839

Nuestra Señora de Belén

AY

Templo de Santiago

A Palencia 52KM

Santa Maria
del Camino

K1

Santa Clara

Puerta y restos
de muralla

Arroyo del Valle

K2

K3

Arroyo del Cubo

K4

Valdefrinilla

K5

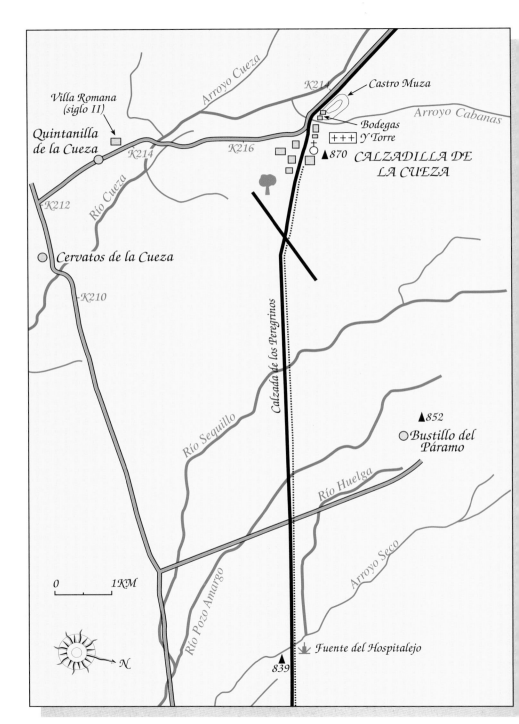

Villa Romana
(siglo II)

Quintanilla
de la Cueza

K214

K212

Río Cueza

Arroyo Cueza

K216

K214

Castro Muza

Bodegas
Y Torre

+ + +

▲870

CALZADILLA DE
LA CUEZA

Arroyo Cabanas

Cervatos de la Cueza

K210

Calzada de los Peregrinos

Río Sequillo

▲852

○Bustillo del
Páramo

Río Huelga

Arroyo Seco

Río Pozo Amargo

0   1KM

N

Fuente del Hospitalejo

▲
839

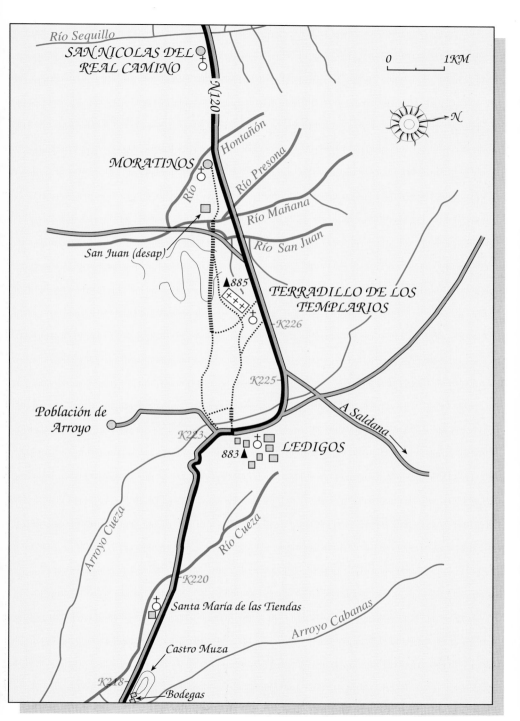

Río Sequillo

SAN NICOLAS DEL
REAL CAMINO

N 120

Hontañón

MORATINOS

Río

Río Presona

Río Mañana

San Juan (desap)

Río San Juan

▲885

TERRADILLO DE LOS
TEMPLARIOS

K226

K225

Población de
Arroyo

K223

883 ▲

LEDIGOS

A Saldana

Arroyo Cueza

Río Cueza

K220

Santa María de las Tiendas

Arroyo Cabanas

Castro Muza

K218

Bodegas

0   1KM

N

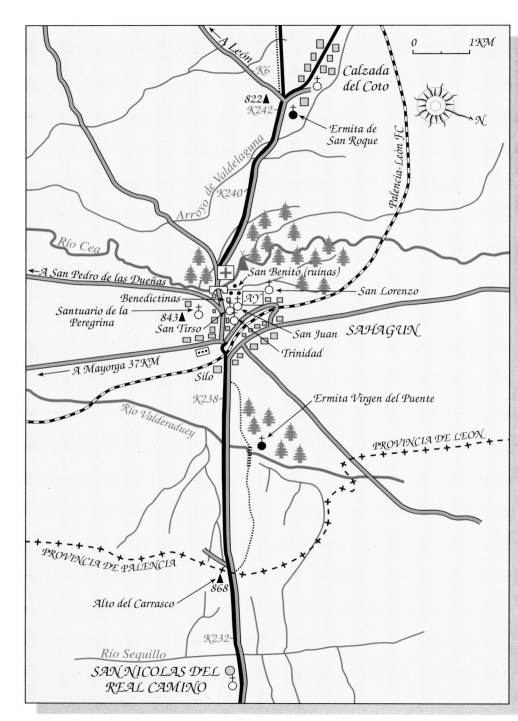

Calzada
del Coto

A León

K6

822▲
K242

Ermita de
San Roque

Palencia-León FC

Arroyo de Valdelaguna

K240

Río Cea

San Benito (ruinas)

A San Pedro de las Dueñas

San Lorenzo

Benedictinas

AY

San Juan

SAHAGUN

Santuario de la
Peregrina

843▲
San Tirso

Trinidad

A Mayorga 37KM

Silo

K238

Ermita Virgen del Puente

Río Valderaduey

PROVINCIA DE LEON

PROVINCIA DE PALENCIA

868▲

Alto del Carrasco

K232

Río Sequillo

SAN NICOLAS DEL
REAL CAMINO

0   1KM

N

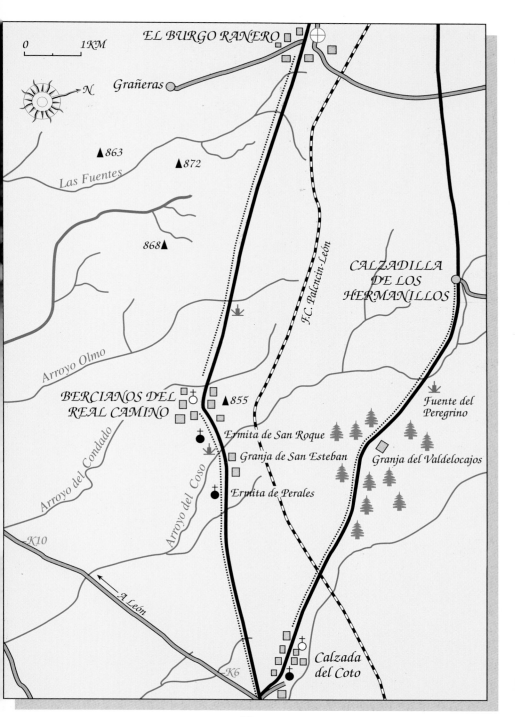

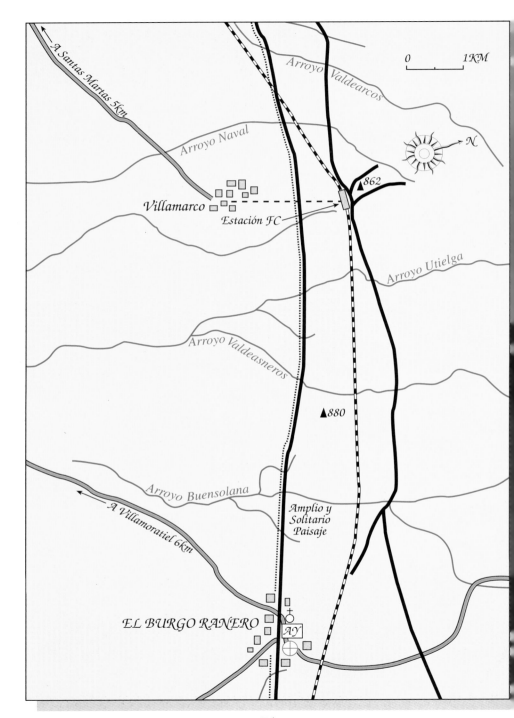

A Santtas Martas 5km

Arroyo Valdearcos

0   1KM

Arroyo Naval

N

▲862

Villamarco

Estación FC

Arroyo Utielga

Arroyo Valdeasneros

▲880

Arroyo Buensolana

Amplio y
Solitario
Paisaje

A Villamoratiel 6km

EL BURGO RANERO

AY

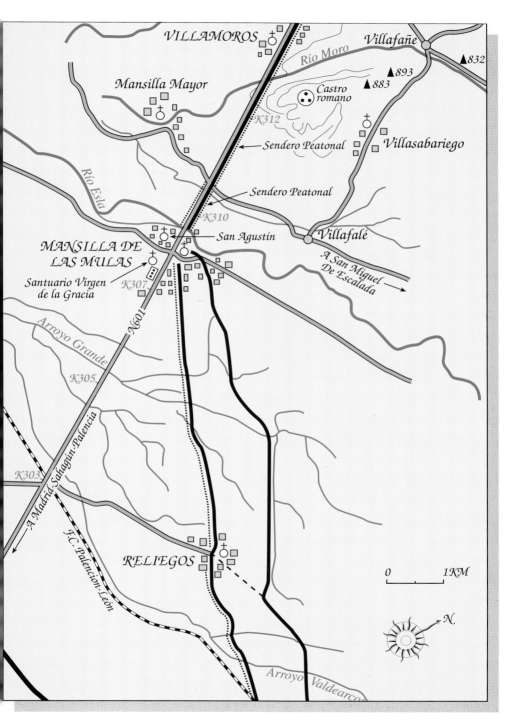

VILLAMOROS

Mansilla Mayor

Río Moro

Villafañe

▲832

▲893

Castro romano

▲883

K312

Villasabariego

Sendero Peatonal

Río Esla

Sendero Peatonal

K310

San Agustín

Villafalé

MANSILLA DE LAS MULAS

A San Miguel De Escalada

Santuario Virgen de la Gracia

K307

Arroyo Grande

N601

K305

A Madrid-Sahagún-Palencia

K303

F.C. Palencia-León

RELIEGOS

0   1KM

N.

Arroyo Valdearcos

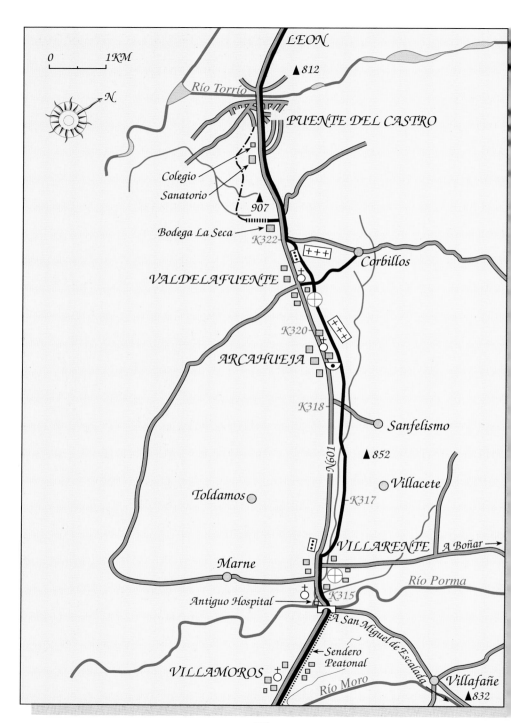

0   1KM

N.

LEON

▲ 812

Río Torrío

PUENTE DEL CASTRO

Colegio
Sanatorio

▲ 907

Bodega La Seca

K322

+ + +

Corbillos

VALDELAFUENTE

⊕

K320

+ + +

ARCAHUEJA

K318

Sanfelismo

▲ 852

N.601

Villacete

K317

Toldamos

VILLARENTE

A Boñar →

Río Porma

Marne

⊕

Antiguo Hospital →

K315

A San Miguel de Escalada

Sendero
Peatonal

VILLAMOROS

Río Moro

Villafañe

▲ 832

76

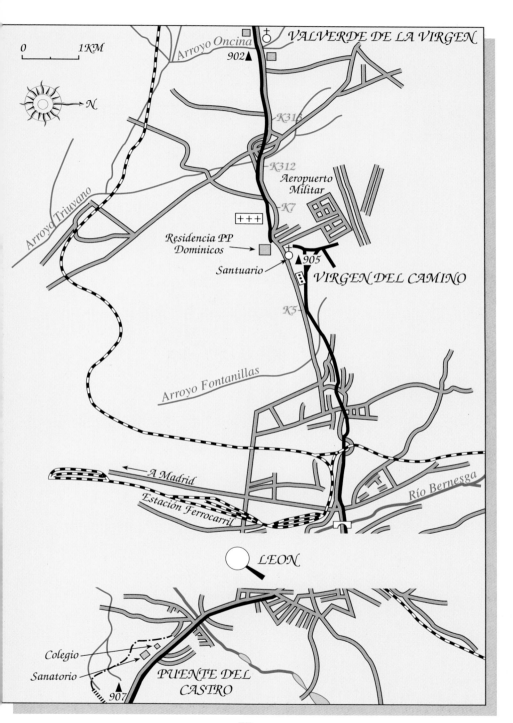

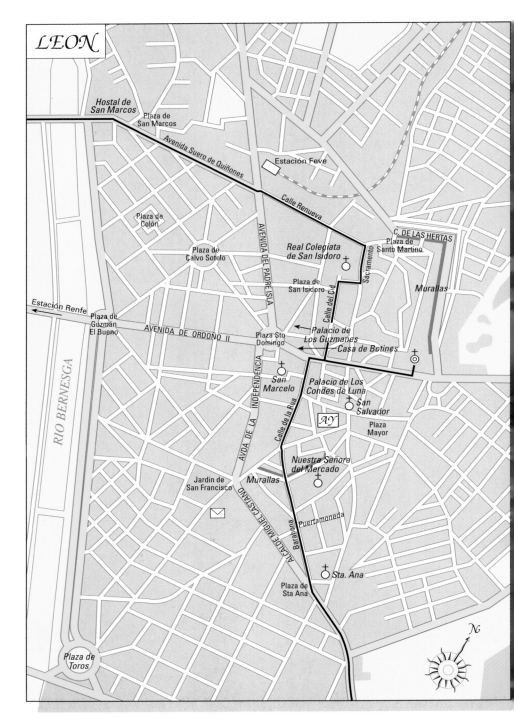

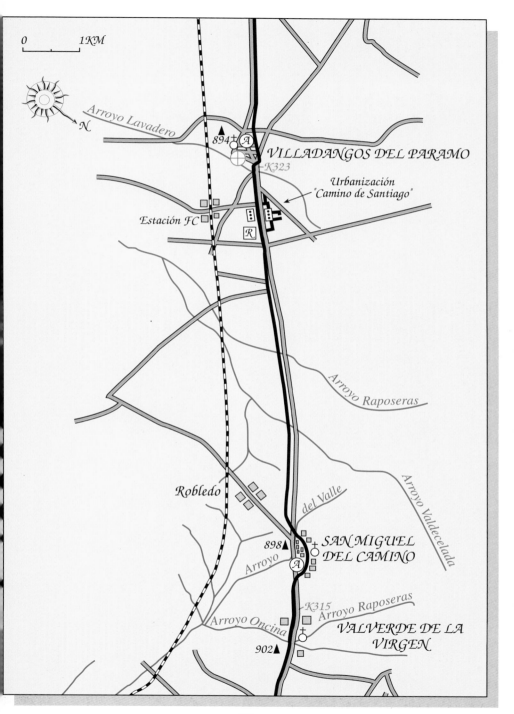

0   1KM

N

Arroyo Lavadero

894 † Ⓐ

VILLADANGOS DEL PÁRAMO

K323

Urbanización
"Camino de Santiago"

Estación FC

Ⓡ

Arroyo Raposeras

Robledo

del Valle

Arroyo Valdecelada

898 ▲

SAN MIGUEL DEL CAMINO

Ⓐ

Arroyo

K315   *Arroyo Raposeras*

Arroyo Oncina

VALVERDE DE LA VIRGEN

902 ▲

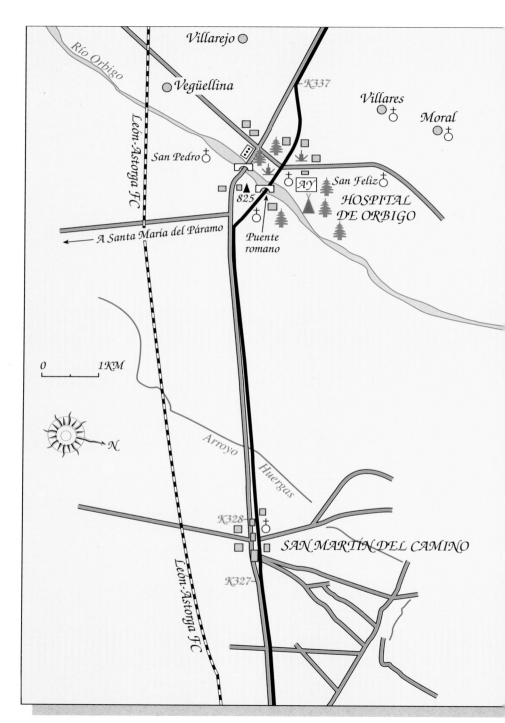

Villarejo

Río Orbigo

Vegüellina

K337

Villares
†

Moral
†

León-Astorga FC

San Pedro †

AY   San Feliz †

HOSPITAL
DE ORBIGO

825

†

A Santa María del Páramo →

Puente
romano

0   1KM

N

Arroyo

Huergas

K328   †

K327

SAN MARTÍN DEL CAMINO

León-Astorga FC

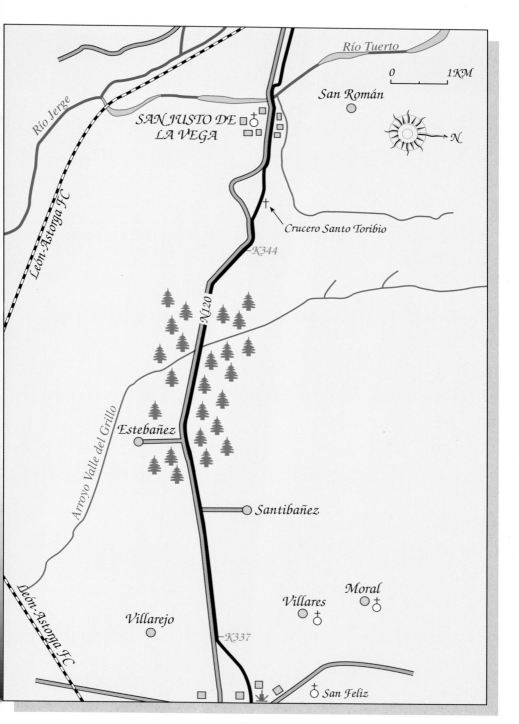

Río Tuerto

Río Jerge

0   1KM

San Román

León-Astorga FC

SAN JUSTO DE
LA VEGA

N

Crucero Santo Toribio

K344

N120

Arroyo Valle del Grillo

Estebañez

Santibañez

Moral

Villares

Villarejo

K337

León-Astorga FC

San Feliz

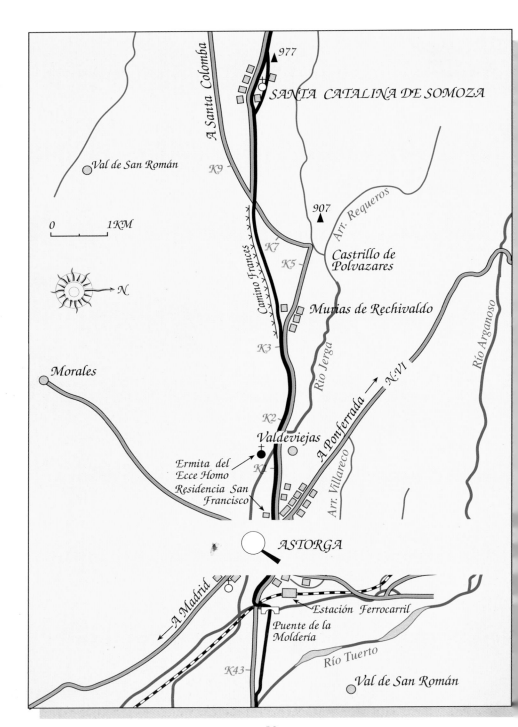

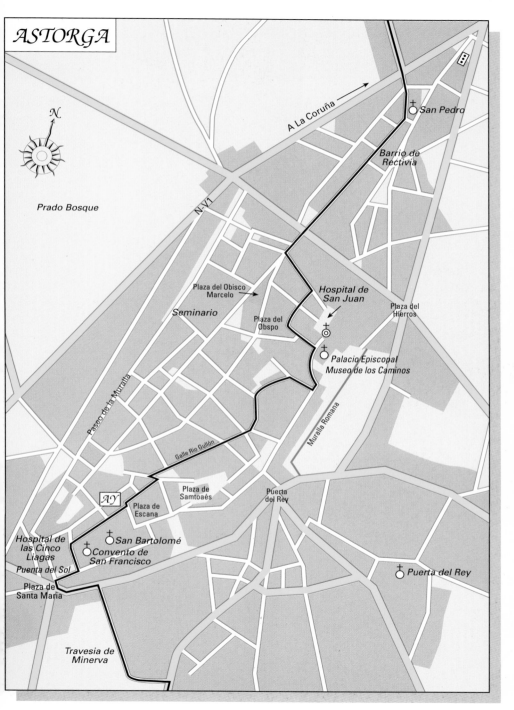

ASTORGA

A La Coruña

San Pedro

Barrio de Rectivia

Prado Bosque

N-VI

Plaza del Obisco Marcelo

Hospital de San Juan

Plaza del Hierros

Seminario

Plaza del Obspo

Palacio Episcopal
Museo de los Caminos

Paseo de la Muralla

Muralla Romana

Galle Rio Gullón

Plaza de Samtoaés

Puerta del Rey

AY

Plaza de Escana

Hospital de las Cinco Liagas

Puenta del Sol

San Bartolomé

Convento de San Francisco

Puerta del Rey

Plaza de Santa Maria

Travesia de Minerva

83

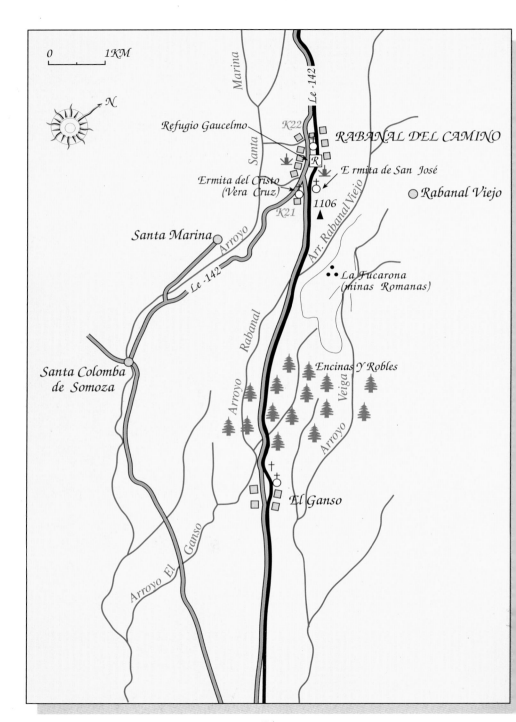

0 1KM

N

Refugio Gaucelmo

K22

RABANAL DEL CAMINO

R

Ermita de San José

Ermita del Cristo
(Vera Cruz)

Rabanal Viejo

1106

K21

Santa Marina

Le -142

La Jucarona
(minas Romanas)

Santa Colomba
de Somoza

Encinas y Robles

El Ganso

Arroyo El Ganso

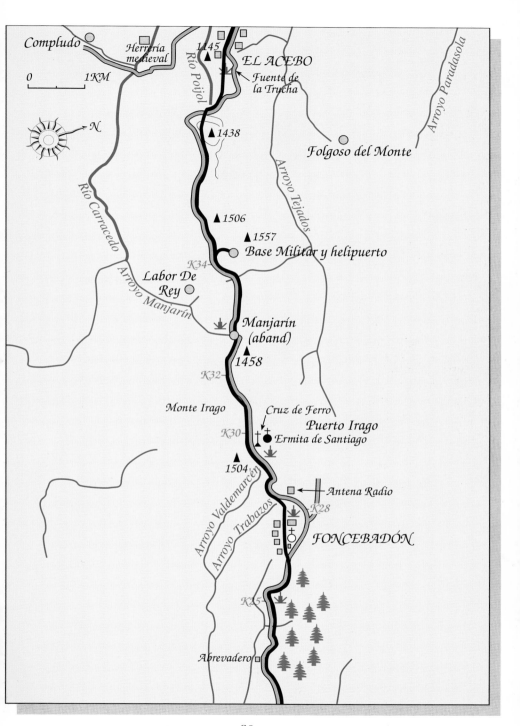

Compludo

Herrería
medieval

0   1KM

N

Río Poijol

1145

EL ACEBO

Fuente de
la Trucha

1438

Folgoso del Monte

Arroyo Paradasola

Arroyo Tejados

Río Carracedo

1506

1557

Base Militar y helipuerto

K34

Arroyo Manjarín

Labor De
Rey

Manjarín
(aband)

1458

K32

Monte Irago

Cruz de Ferro

Puerto Irago

K30

Ermita de Santiago

1504

Antena Radio

Arroyo Valdemarcén

Arroyo Trabazos

K28

FONCEBADÓN

K25

Abrevadero

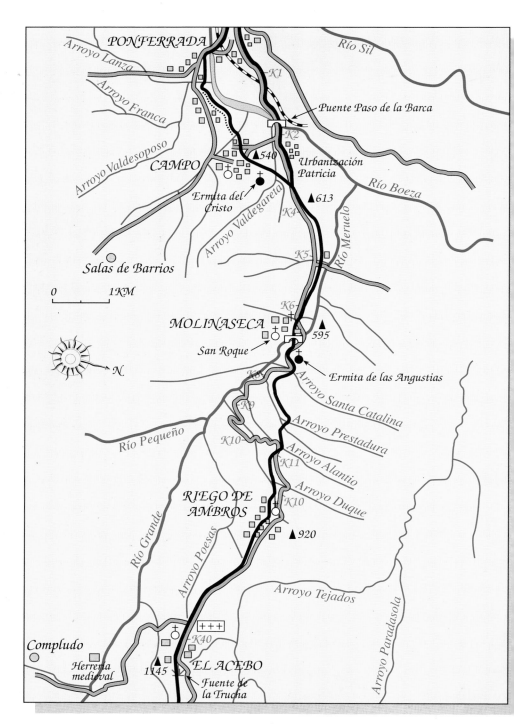

PONFERRADA

Arroyo Lanza

Arroyo Franca

Río Sil

K1

Puente Paso de la Barca

K2

Arroyo Valdesoposo

CAMPO

▲540

Urbanización
Patricia

Río Boeza

Ermita del
Cristo

Arroyo Valdegareta

▲613

K4

Río Meruelo

K5

Salas de Barrios

0   1KM

N

MOLINASECA

K6

▲
595

San Roque

Ermita de las Angustias

K8

Arroyo Santa Catalina

K9

Arroyo Prestadura

Río Pequeño

K10

Arroyo Alantio

K11

RIEGO DE
AMBROS

K10

Arroyo Duque

Arroyo Poesas

▲920

Río Grande

Arroyo Tejados

Arroyo Paradasola

Compludo

+ + +

K40

Herrería
medieval

▲
1145

EL ACEBO

Fuente de
la Trucha

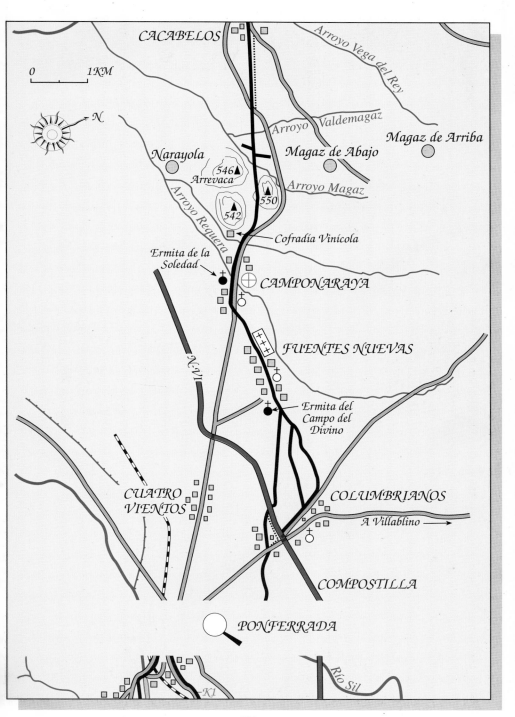

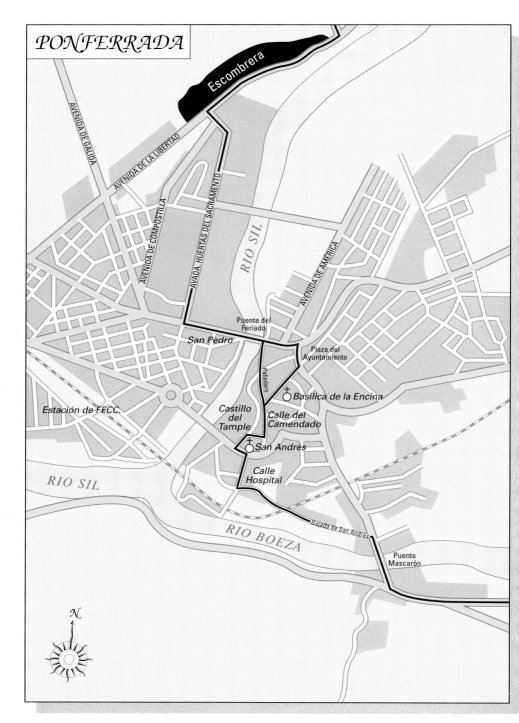

PONFERRADA

Escombrera

AVENIDA DE GALIDA

AVENIDA DE LA LIBERTAD

AVENIDA DE COMPOSTILLA

AVDA. HUERTAS DEL SACRAMENTO

RIO SIL

AVENIDA DE AMÉRICA

Puente del Feriado

San Pedro

Plaza del Ayuntamiento

Rañedero

Basílica de la Encina

Estación de FFCC.

Castillo del Tample

Calle del Camendado

San Andrés

Calle Hospital

RIO SIL

RIO BOEZA

Bajada de San Andrés

Puente Mascarón

N

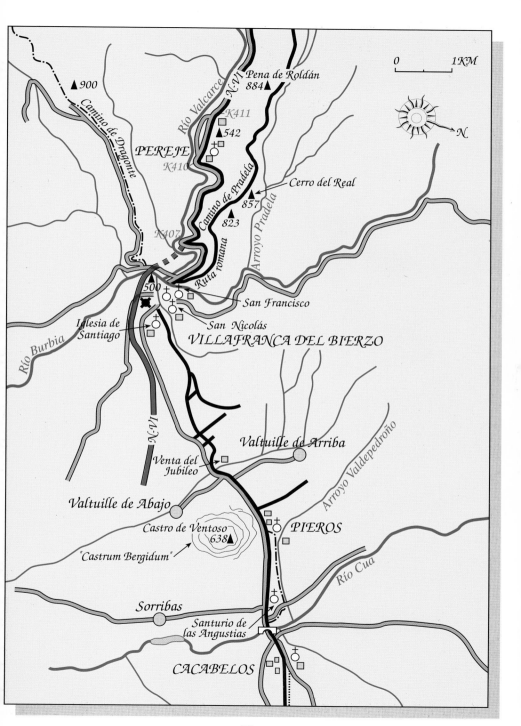

0   1KM

N

▲ 900

Camino de Dragonte

Río Valcarce

Pena de Roldán
884▲

K411

▲542

PEREJE

K410

Camino de Pradela

Cerro del Real

857▲

823

Arroyo Pradela

K407

Ruta romana

500
San Francisco

San Nicolás

Iglesia de
Santiago

Río Burbia

VILLAFRANCA DEL BIERZO

N-VI

Valtuille de Arriba

Venta del
Jubileo

Arroyo Valdepedroño

Valtuille de Abajo

Castro de Ventoso
638▲

PIEROS

"Castrum Bergidum"

Río Cua

Sorribas

Santurio de
las Angustias

CACABELOS

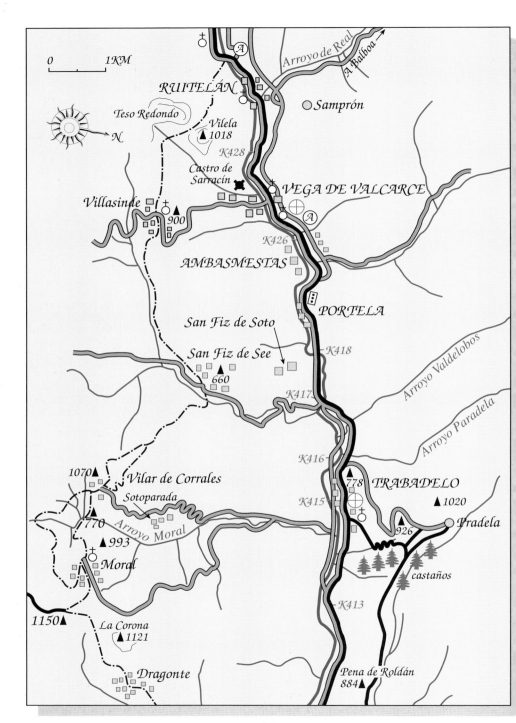

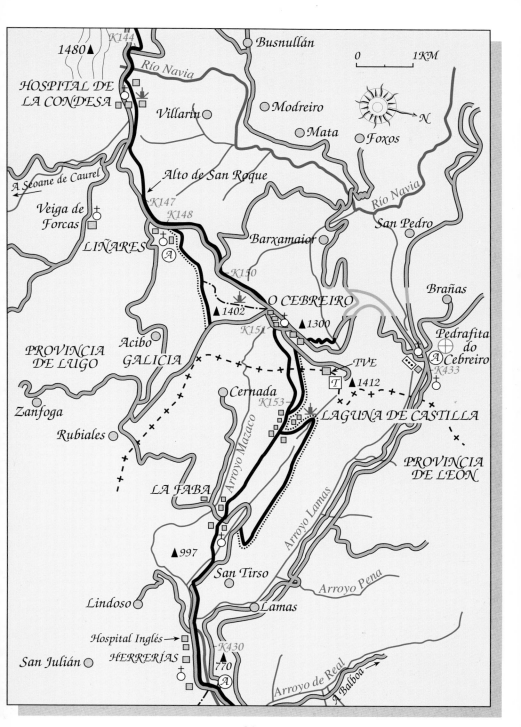

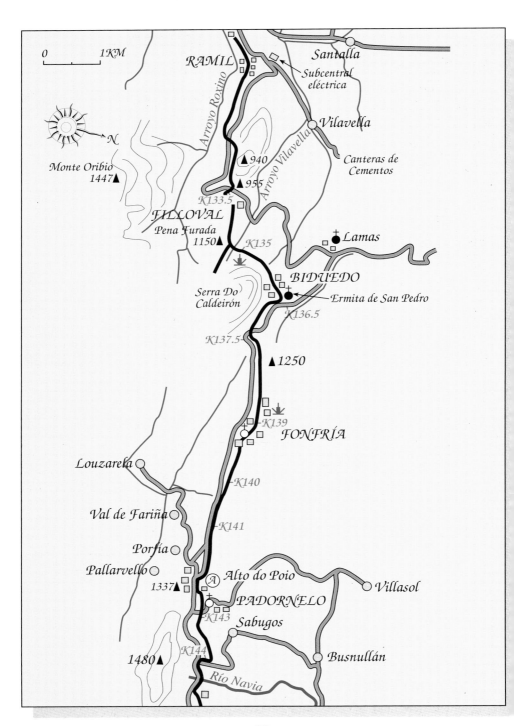

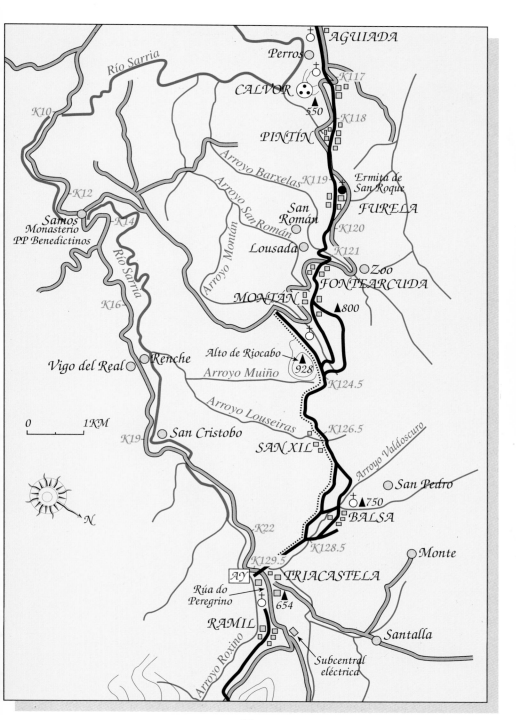

Río Sarria

K10

K12

Samos
Monasterio
PP Benedictinos

K14

Río Sarria

K16

Vigo del Real

Renche

0   1KM

N

K19   San Cristobo

K22

RAMIL

Arroyo Roxino

AGUIADA

Perros

K117

CALVOR

550

K118

PINTÍN

Arroyo Barxelas   K119

Ermita de
San Roque

FURELA

San
Román

Arroyo San Román

K120

Lousada

K121

Arroyo Montán

Zoo

FONTEARCUDA

MONTÁN

800

Alto de Riocabo

928

Arroyo Muiño

K124.5

Arroyo Louseiras

K126.5

SAN XIL

Arroyo Valdoscuro

San Pedro

750

BALSA

K128.5

Monte

K129.5

AY   TRIACASTELA

Rúa do
Peregrino

654

Subcentral
eléctrica

Santalla

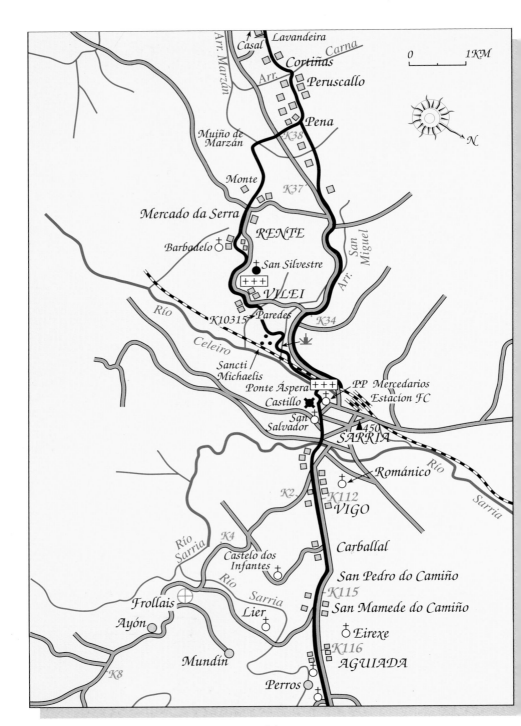

0   1KM

Lavandeira
Casal
Cortiñas
Carna
Arr. Marzán
Arr.
Peruscallo
N
Pena
K38
Muiño de
Marzán
Monte
K37
Mercado da Serra
RENTE
San Miguel
Barbadelo
San Silvestre
+++
VILEI
Río
K10315
Paredes
K34
Arr.
Celeiro
Sancti
Michaelis
Ponte Áspera
+++
PP Mercedarios
Castillo
Estación FC
San
Salvador
450
SARRIA
Río
Románico
Sarria
K2
K112
VIGO
Río
Sarria
K4
Carballal
Castelo dos
Infantes
San Pedro do Camiño
Frollais
Sarria
Río
K115
San Mamede do Camiño
Ayón
Lier
Eirexe
K116
Mundín
AGUIADA
K8
Perros

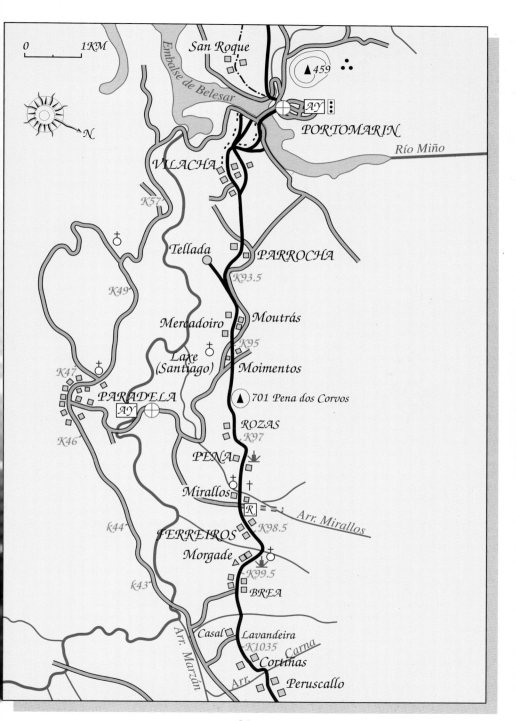

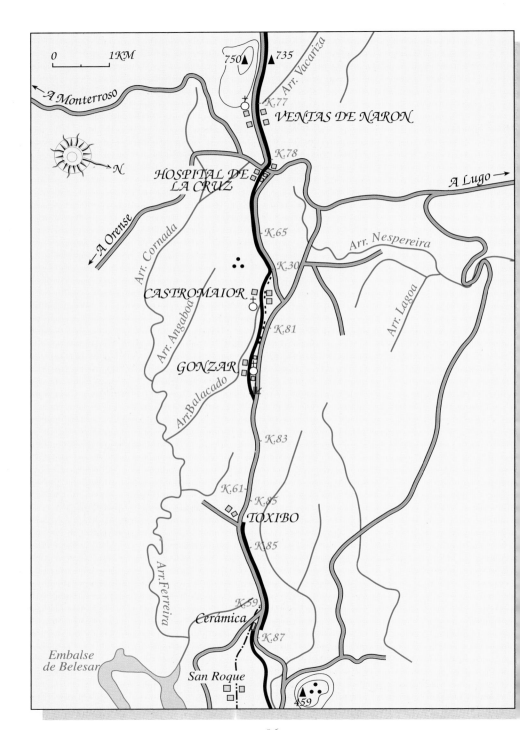

0   1KM

A Monterroso

N

750 ▲   ▲ 735

Arr. Vacariza

K.77

VENTAS DE NARON

K.78

HOSPITAL DE LA CRUZ

A Lugo →

A Orense

Arr. Cornada

K.65

K.30

Arr. Nespereira

CASTROMAIOR

Arr. Angaboa

K.81

Arr. Lagoa

GONZAR

Arr. Balacado

K.83

K.61

K.85

TOXIBO

K.185

Arr. Ferreira

K.59

Cerámica

K.87

Embalse de Belesar

San Roque

459

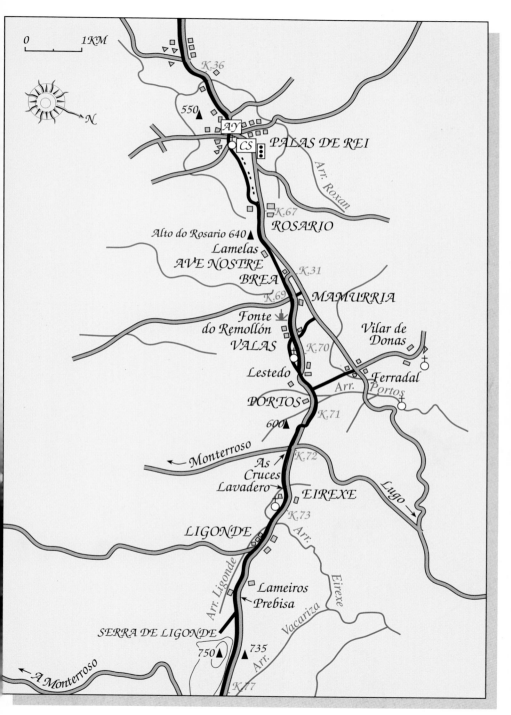

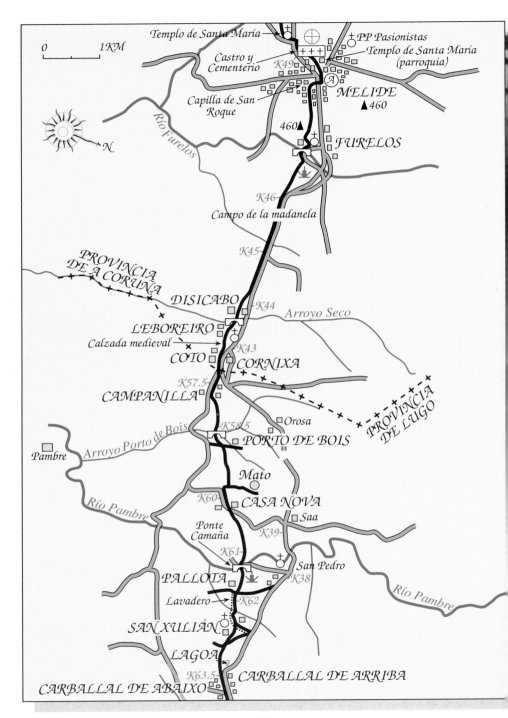

Templo de Santa María

PP Pasionistas

Templo de Santa María
(parroquia)

Castro y
Cementerio

K49

MELIDE
▲460

Capilla de San
Roque

460▲

FURELOS

Río Furelos

K46

Campo de la madanela

K45

PROVINCIA
DE A CORUÑA

DISICABO

K44

Arroyo Seco

LEBOREIRO

Calzada medieval

K43

COTO

CORNIXA

K57.5

CAMPANILLA

PROVINCIA
DE LUGO

K58.5

Orosa

Pambre

Arroyo Porto de Bois

PORTO DE BOIS

Mato

Río Pambre

K60

CASA NOVA

Saa

Ponte
Camaña

K39

K61

San Pedro

PALLOTA

K38

Lavadero

K62

Río Pambre

SAN XULIÁN

LAGOA

K63.5

CARBALLAL DE ARRIBA

CARBALLAL DE ABAIXO

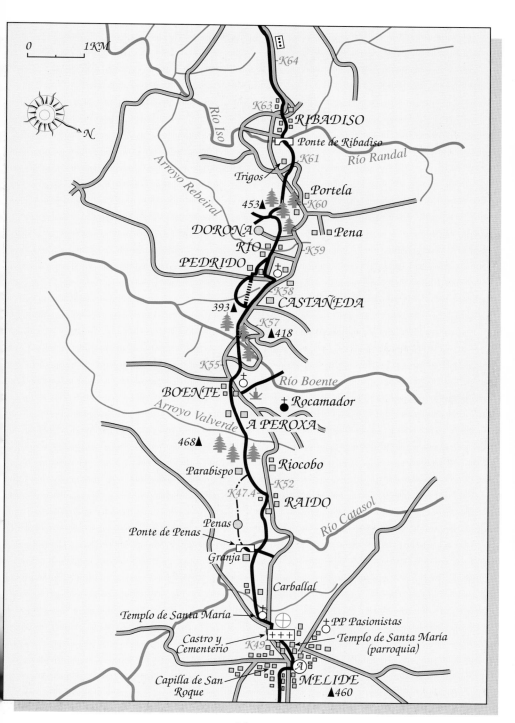

0   1KM

N

K64

K63

RIBADISO

Ponte de Ribadiso

K61   *Río Randal*

Trigos

Portela

453▲   K60

Río Iso

Arroyo Rebeiral

DORONA   *Pena*

RÍO   K59

PEDRIDO

K58

393▲   *CASTAÑEDA*

K57

▲418

K55

Río Boente

BOENTE

Rocamador

Arroyo Valverde   *A PEROXA*

468▲

Riocobo

Parabispo   K52

K47.4

RAIDO

Río Catasol

Penas

Ponte de Penas

Granja

Carballal

Templo de Santa María

PP *Pasionistas*

Castro y
Cementerio   K49   *Templo de Santa María*
                    (parroquia)

A

Capilla de San   *MELIDE*
Roque   ▲460

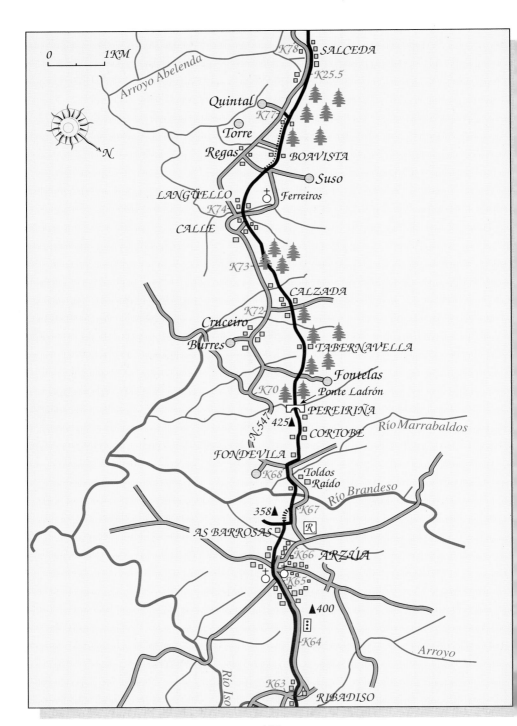

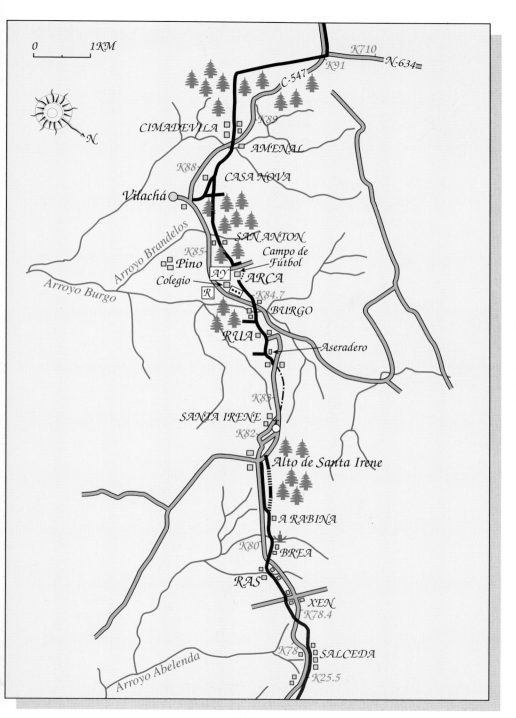

SANTIAGO DE COMPOSTELA

0   1KM

N

SAN LAZARO

K720

K719

Autopista A-9

N-634

Monte do Gozo
(Monxoi)   368▲
SAN MARCOS

K718

K717

▲391

A Zamarrazedo   TVE

TVG   K716

K715

Fonte dos
Pelamios

San Roque

VILAMAYOR

LAVACOLLA

Colegio

A Sigüero

K713

K93

SAN PAIO

K711

K712

Aeropuerto

K710

K91

N-634

C-547

102

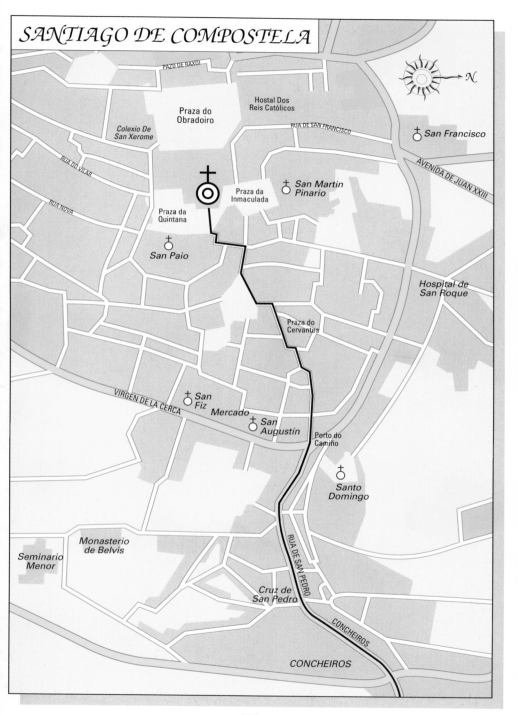

SANTIAGO DE COMPOSTELA

PAZO DE RAXOI

Praza do
Obradoiro

Hostal Dos
Reis Católicos

Colexio De
San Xerome

RUA DE SAN FRANCISCO

San Francisco

AVENIDA DE JUAN XXIII

RUA DO VILAR

Praza da
Inmaculada

San Martin
Pinario

RUA NOVA

Praza da
Quintana

San Paio

Hospital de
San Roque

Praza do
Cervantes

VIRGEN DE LA CERCA

San
Fiz

Mercado

San
Augustín

Porto do
Camiño

Santo
Domingo

Monasterio
de Belvis

Seminario
Menor

RUA DE SAN PEDRO

Cruz de
San Pedro

CONCHEIROS

CONCHEIROS

Refugios for Pilgrims on the Camino de Santiago

Navarra		Tel: Area Code 948
Roncesvalles	Real Colegiata	76 00 00
Zubiri	Ayuntamiento, Parroquia	30 40 71
Larrasoaña	Ayuntamiento	30 42 42
Trinidad de Arre	Convento de la Trinidad	11 06 79
Villava	Círculo Carlista	
Pamplona	Asociación de Amigos del Camino	
	Blas de la Serna, 58-1°	24 09 75
	Ayuntamiento	22 12 00
Cizur Menor	Familia Roncal	18 38 85
Puenta la Reina	P.P. Reparadores	34 00 50
Estella	Ayuntamiento	54 63 63
Los Arcos	Parroquia	64 00 79
Torres del Río	Casa Santa Bárbara	64 80 06
	Parroquia	64 81 57
Viana	Parroquia, Plaza de Serapio Mora	64 50 37

La Rioja		Tel: Area Code 941
Logroño	Refugio de la JOC. Calle del Hospital	
	Viejo 9, bajo. Parroquia de	
	San Bartolomé	26 00 01
	F.M. de la Paz	
	Rodríguez Paterna 5	25 06 03
Navarette	Parroquia	44 00 17
	P.P. Camilos	44 00 87
Nájera	P.P. Franciscanos de Santa	
	María La Real	36 36 50
Azofra	Parroquia	37 90 63
Santo Domingo de la		
Calzada	Casa del Santo	34 33 90
Grañon	Parroquia	34 26 09

Burgos		Tel: Area Code 947
Redicilla del Camino	Parroquia	58 81 23

Convent and pilgrim refuge at Trinidad de Arre near Pamplona.

Castildelgado	Ayuntamiento	58 80 75
Belorado	Parroquia	58 00 85
Villafranca Montes de Oca	Ayuntamiento	58 01 72
San Juan de Ortega	Monasterio	43 80 16
Rubena	Parroquia	43 10 09
Burgos	Ayuntamiento	23 44 00
	Colegio Menor	22 54 00
	Seminario	20 52 47
Villalbilla	Ayuntamiento	20 38 57
Tardajos	Ayuntamiento	45 11 89
Hornillos del Camino	Ayuntamiento	41 10 50
Hontanas	Ayuntamiento	37 70 35
Castrojeríz	Asociación de Amigos	37 70 34
	Parroquia	37 70 36

Palencia

Itero de la Vega	Ayuntamiento	15 18 26
Boadilla del Camino	Ayuntamiento	81 03 90
Frómista	Parroquia	81 01 44
	Ayuntamiento	81 00 01
Población de Campos	Ayuntamiento	81 02 93
Villalcázar de Sirga	Parroquia	88 80 76
	Mesón Pablo Payo	88 80 22
Carrión de los Condes	Parroquia de Sta. María del Camino	88 00 72
	Ayuntamiento	88 02 59
Ledigos	Ayuntamiento	88 30 30

León

Sahagún	Hermanos de la Caridad	78 00 85
	Ayuntamiento	78 00 01
Calzada del Coto	Ayuntamiento	78 12 33
Bercianos del Real Camino	Parroquia	78 41 22
	Ayuntamiento	78 42 59
El Burgo Ranero	Ayuntamiento	33 00 23
Villamarco	Ayuntamiento	31 41 70
Reliegos	Ayuntamiento	31 78 55
Mansilla de las Mulas	Ayuntamiento	31 09 41
Villarente	Parroquia	31 23 27
León	Ayuntamiento	22 31 00
	Real Colegiata de San Isidoro	23 66 00
	MM Benedictinas	25 28 66
San Miguel del Camino	Ayuntamiento	30 01 31
Villadangos del Páramo	Ayuntamiento	39 00 03
Hospital de Orbigo	Parroquia	38 84 44
	Ayuntamiento	38 82 06
San Justo de la Vega	Parroquia	61 59 26
Astorga	Colegio Cosamai	61 59 76
Murias de Rechivaldo	Junta Vecinal	61 51 58
Rabanal del Camino	Refugio Gaucelmo	63 94 68
	Parroquia	61 52 03
El Acebo	Junta Vecinal	41 42 92
Molinaseca	Parroquia	41 98 03

Ponferrada	Basilica de la Encina	41 19 78
Columbrianos	Parroquia	41 39 61
Camponaraya	Parroquia	46 30 42
Cacabelos	Parroquia	54 61 10
Villafranca del Bierzo	Familia Jato, adjacent to la Iglesia de Santiago	54 02 29
	Parroquia	54 00 80
	Ayuntamiento	54 00 89
Vega de Valcarce	Bar Español	54 31 13
Herrerías	Señor Urbano	

Lugo		**Tel: Area Code 982**
O Cebreiro	Hospedería	36 90 25
O Poio	Mesón O Poio	36 90 67
Triacastela	Ayuntamiento	54 70 47
Samos	Monasterio P.P. Benedictinos	54 60 46
Sarria	P.P. Mercedarios	53 10 20
Ferreiros	Ayuntamiento	54 20 01
Portomarín	Parroquia	54 50 65
	Ayuntamiento	54 50 70
Palas de Rey	Parroquia	38 00 21
	Ayuntamiento	38 00 01

La Coruña		**Tel: Area Code 981**
Leboreiro	Ayuntamiento	50 50 03
Melide	Parroquia	50 51 20
Arzúa	Parroquia	50 05 56
	Ayuntamiento	50 00 00
Arca	Parroquia	51 10 03
	Ayuntamiento	51 10 02
Santiago de Compostela	P.P. Franciscanos	58 16 00
	Seminario Menor de Belvis	58 92 00

The Yesa reservoir and the ruined castle of Ruesta.

NOTE:

1.   Those pilgrims who commence their pilgrimage via the Somport Pass have the possibility of staying in the following refugios:

Canfranc: mountain refuge; Berdún: refugio; Sigüés: refugio; Esco: shelter; Sangüesa: refugio; Monreal: local school. In all cases enquire at the Parroquia, (parish church or house), the Ayuntamiento (Town Hall), or among the local people.

2.   There is an office in the Cathedral of Santiago which welcomes pilgrims and issues the Compostela, the certificate of their pilgrimage. It is situated in the Praza da Quintana, at the east end of the Cathedral, near to the Puerta Santa or Holy Door.

3.   At noon each day Mass is celebrated in the Cathedral of Santiago for all those pilgrims who have presented themselves that day.

4.   For the Holy Year 1993 new refugios are planned in the following places: O Cebreiro, Hospital de la Condesa, (8 km after O Cebreiro), Calvor, (a little before Sarria), Barbadelo, (10 km after Sarria), Gonzar, (4 km after Portomarín), Ventas de Naron, (10 km further on), Ligonde, (3 km more), Lestedo, (before Palas De Rey), Mato, (between Palas and Mellid), Santa Irene, (near to Arca).

Check in advance and in all cases consult the local people on the status of these refugios.

Glossary of Spanish words found on maps

Note: (g) denotes Gallego

a	to	covento	convent
abadía	abbey	corona	crown/hilltop
abandonado (aband.)	abandoned	corral	enclosure
		cruz/cruceiro(g)	cross
aeropuerto	airport	cuartel	barracks
albergue juvenil	youth hostel	de	from, of
alto	height, hill	desaparecido (desap.)	disappeared
antiguo	ancient		
arroyo	brook, stream	desviación	detour/ diversion
aserradero	sawmill	dique	barrier, dyke
autopista	motorway	embalse	reservoir
avenida (avda.)	avenue	encina	holm oak
barrio	neighbourhood, district	ermita	hermitage, chapel
caído	fallen	estación	station
calle	street	granja	farmhouse
camino/ camiño(g)	way, road	FC/ferrocarril	railway
		finca	estate, farmstead
campo	field		
capilla	chapel	fortaleza	fortress
carretera	main road	frontera	frontier
casa, casita	house, small house	frontón	pelota court
		fuente/fonte(g)	fountain, spring
castillo	castle		
catedral	cathedral	gotíco/a	gothic
cementario	cemetery	herrería	smithy, forge
cerámica	pottery, ceramics	huerta	large garden, market garden
chopo	poplar tree	iglesia	church
circumvalación	bypass	madres	mothers (religious)
ciudadela	citadel		
colegio/colexio(g)	school, college	medieval	mediaeval

mercado	market	puente	bridge
militar	military	puerto	pass
mina(s)	mine(s)	real	royal
molina	mill	río	river
monte	mount, mountain	roble	oak
monumento	monument	románico/a	romanesque
museo	museum	rúa	street
Nuesta Señora	Our Lady	ruínas	ruins
oratorio	oratory	san, santo, santa	saint
palacio	palace	seminario	seminary
panadería	bread shop	sendero	path, track
pantano	reservoir, swamp	sierra	range of hills
parque	park		or mountains
pazo(g)	manor house	silo	silo, grainstore
peatonal	pedestrian	torre	tower
pista	track, path	travesía	cross street
plaza/praza(g)	square	urbanización	housing estate,
portal, puerta	door		built up area
pozo	well	viejo/a	old
PP, padres	fathers (religious)	viña	vineyard
provincia	province	zona	zone, area

Index